C000155417

Naomi Hefter

HEF OFF

A Memoir of a Chaotic Comedian

AUSTIN MACAULEY PUBLISHERS™

LONDON • CAMBRIDGE • NEW YORK • SHARJAH

Copyright © Naomi Hefter (2019)

The right of Naomi Hefter to be identified as author of this work has been asserted by her in accordance with section 77 and 78 of the Copyright, Designs and Patents Act 1988.

All rights reserved. No part of this publication may be reproduced, stored in a retrieval system or transmitted in any form or by any means, electronic, mechanical, photocopying, recording or otherwise, without the prior permission of the publishers.

Any person who commits any unauthorised act in relation to this publication may be liable to criminal prosecution and civil claims for damages.

A CIP catalogue record for this title is available from the British Library.

ISBN 9781788780643 (Paperback)
ISBN 9781788780650 (Hardback)
ISBN 9781528955072 (ePub e-book)

www.austinmacauley.com

First Published (2019)
Austin Macauley Publishers Ltd
25 Canada Square
Canary Wharf
London
E14 5LQ

To those who spent the time getting to know me instead of judging me.

Contents

Introduction

CHOOSE LIFE, choose getting fired, choose beating the system, fucking the system, fuck the system. Choose office politics, small talk, polite talk. Signing birthday cards for people you don't even like. Choose snacking because you are bored, eating cake because it's there. Filling up the coffee machine, smiling once you've done it. Choose getting praise for work you hate, hating work for people's praise. Getting paid, having a budget. Working the system, becoming the system. Turning into a robot to suit society. Choose following the rules, breaking rules, feeling like you're back at school. Rules and regulations. Wearing a tie, holding a briefcase. Choose doing what you really love. Life is too short. Do what makes you happy. Use your brain, get creative. Be expressive. Be who you want to be. Do what you want to do. CHOOSE YOUR FUTURE—CHOOSE GETTING FIRED.

They say there is a very thin line between comedy and tragedy.

Within the space of a few years, I had been fired 36 times, been arrested 3 times and wet myself in Topshop. I had been diagnosed with depression, post-traumatic stress and anxiety.

I received counselling for anger management and cognitive behavioural therapy before being referred for psychotherapy.

The worst part was, I had also lost the love of my life.

It wasn't until August 2009 when I had hit rock bottom.

I reached the point where I had no money, couldn't get a job and I was shoplifting at an uncontrollable rate.

Having lost all direction of where I was going in life, I only had two simple choices left. I could literally give up all hope, or I could keep on going and find something to focus on. I opted with the latter. But there was a long dark, rocky, emotional road ahead, with many unexpected surprises to come before things were good again.

This is my memoir. It was not written to become self-indulgent or contrived. This is just my story to share with anyone who can relate to heartbreak, hating their job or finding themselves in a dark place where they feel there is no way out.

My name is Naomi Hefter. You probably have no idea who I am. But you will.

2009

The Honest Thief

Diary Extract – August 10, 2009

As I slipped the most expensive pack of Marks and Spencer's Scottish smoked salmon into the September issue of Vogue magazine, I suddenly thought it was packed flat enough to almost look like a free sample of fish that had been put inside already for readers to try. The glossy pages of Vogue already came with a sample of shampoo and expensive foundation, after all. Holding the iconic magazine under my arm, like the bankers in the city held their daily newspapers, I almost looked like a wealthy girl in the capital with my perfectly liquid-lined eyes and nude matte lips. As I walked out of the shop on Oxford Street, having not paid for my 'sample of dinner', I felt surprisingly calm. Vogue was also unpaid for. I left the shop without getting caught.

The first time I shoplifted, I was 13 when I went through that shit with Bill. But this time, it wasn't just because I was desperately unhappy. This was because I had £2.67 in my bank account and I had lost over a stone in weight since I had gotten fired last month. And if I was going to steal my dinner, I was, at least, going to steal an expensive piece of fish to help ease the hunger pains in my frail body. And I had a magazine to read too...

If someone had told me years ago that I would one day steal so much smoked salmon I would be giving it away to the homeless, I would have laughed. But as it turned out, I did steal stupid amounts of the fish, and I did give plenty to the homeless. One thing is for sure, I can never look at that flat packed packet of fish in the same way again. I just hope those homeless people at Charing Cross station enjoyed the smoked salmon as much as I did at one stage.

On January 1, 2009, it was an unusually warm day. I remember looking up at the sky and seeing nothing but a gigantic swirl of muddled, grey clouds that covered my world. As I wheeled two large suitcases down the street, from one shared flat to another, I stopped for a moment and felt pure stillness surround me, but sheer panic swamped and filled me with dread of where my life was now going. When most people were in bed with a stinking hangover, I had packed up my belongings and walked my whole life down from one end to the other on Stoke Newington Church Street, to move in with new roommates that I had met through Gumtree.

I had been living with my boyfriend, David, in Stoke Newington, North London, since we moved from Bristol in 2007. After a year of living in London together, things had gone severely downhill. Not knowing anyone or anything in the vast capital city put immense pressure on our relationship. That and the fact that I was not in the right time in my life to be in a relationship. Over the years prior to meeting David, I had been offered anger management, counselling, and was put on a year's waiting list to have cognitive behavioural therapy. I never showed up to my first CBT appointment, which was two days before my 23rd birthday.

Seven months after I turned 23, December 2, 2006, was a day that ultimately changed my life forever. I had broken up with my first and only boyfriend after I had asked myself the question that probably everybody asks themselves at one point in their lives, "Could I see myself with this person 10, even 5 years from now?" I couldn't. We were very different people. I wanted life in the big city of London and he was happy to live a modest life in his home town of Worcester. So, I ended it, clean and simple, and we remained friends after the initial sting of surprise he felt had passed.

Living in Bristol as a 23-year-old, and saving to move to London, I was having fun, living the life of any normal 23-

year-old should. I was living with not one, but FIVE 21-year-old guys. It was something I wasn't used to, as not only was I an only child until I was 13 but I had also only lived with girls during university. Living with these boisterous guys was carnage. Charts up on the wall, with scoring points on who fucked the most girls, with minus points for bringing back a girl and not doing anything with them, as if they ever admit to such a thing! Porn films and video games scattered over the entire living room floor, three giant fridge freezers stacked full of Jack Daniels and beer. There were countless house parties, with endless supplies of cheap sugary WKD drinks and frozen pizzas cooking away in the oven. Old girlfriends and new girls would be invited amongst so many other guys and girls. One night during another busy gathering at the house, an ex-girlfriend of one of my roommates came around, and had been calling me names and threatened to 'sort me out', making assumptions I fancied him. Later that night, she was formerly introduced to me, and I simply put my hand out to shake hers and affirmed, "Oh, hello. You're the girl who called me a slag and is going to sort me out, pleased to meet you."

You could have heard a pin drop in the entire house, as she didn't know what to reply with as her face froze in surprise. There was a time in my life where I felt fearless. I was tenacious and would say whatever was on my mind. I felt no intimidation, no worries and nothing stood in my way. But any self-belief in anything good ever happening to me in life was never there.

Days living with five carefree lads were fun but being outnumbered was difficult and it was often hard to keep up with their antics. One of the housemates, Louis, I got on well with due to our mutual love of dance music and ambition to make it big in the world. So, on a spontaneous night out, on that frosty December night, wearing nothing more than a pair of teeny tiny black shorts and a tight black top that covered my arms, and wrapped about my boobs that left nothing to the imagination. We walked into Oceana nightclub in the heart of Bristol with, and were both determined to appear single and not an item or on a date, which was ironic considering that I met the love of my life that night. Louis and I had literally been inside the huge club for less than ten minutes queuing to buy our first drink, when I saw him. The One. People often don't believe in love at first sight. But it exists. I am living proof. I had always considered myself a cynical person on the outside, believing things only when I saw or experienced them myself. But underneath it all, the people who really knew me knew that I was a hopeless romantic who wore my heart on my sleeve. I believed in happy endings, but it was the prospect of that ever happening to me left me feeling vulnerable and slightly uncomfortable because of the childhood I had experienced.

The only way I could ever describe love at first sight is that I felt a shift in my life, a sudden change. I remember vividly looking at the side of his face and nothing else in that moment mattered in life. When I saw him, it was as though something was finalised. I didn't need to look any further. That person, a stranger to me, was the only one in the room. All images, all sounds, all movements stopped. Everyone around him had become blurred. My brain, my instincts and my heart spoke out, shouting at me that this was it. It was an overwhelming sense that I had undoubtedly, right in that moment, found The One. I just knew I was going to marry that person standing in front of me and I didn't even know his name.

I always hated that cliché line that you find your one true love once you stop looking, but as far as I was concerned, once it happened, I had to agree with all those others who had experienced the same thing. I was left in a trance like state but within moments, I was zoomed back out into the room and he had disappeared into the crowd. But I knew I would see him again. Lo and behold, later that night, I saw him walking through the crowded dance floor and it was then I had to approach him.

I took the cheesy approach and decided to dance near him to catch his attention. Trying my Shakira style sexy hip moves, I swayed, swirled, and gyrated closer and closer. My hip popping attempts were quickly put to bed once I realised, I looked like I could easily break my pelvic bone and lose all dignity. The very first thing I asked him was what his star sign was, and I noticed he was wearing the fragrance Romance by Calvin Klein because everyone was wearing it at that time. Within minutes, I discovered David was 24, single and had his own little flat just outside of Bristol city centre. There was instant chemistry as we chatted away and danced; so only an hour later, but what felt like days but yet only a few minutes too, I kissed David right there and then. I remember so clearly as we kissed our teeth banged against each other's, but it still just felt right. But on that very first night of David meeting me, a flash of what was to come had entered his life. The chaos and mayhem that I constantly carried with me was about to be introduced to him… Out of nowhere, I suddenly found myself knocked out unconscious on the dance floor. An unexpected fist had landed SMACK on my nose as I was fiercely punched by a girl who had tried to dance with David. The moment this person, this stranger had made the decision to dance in between David and I, it was my inner demon who was not confident enough inside to handle the competition, felt attacked and vulnerable. This was a problem I had faced for years. A confident calming exterior of a swan, with frantic, fast paddled legs that flapped and thrashed underneath that no one could see. That was me. So, puffing out my chest and tapping her on the shoulder, I defensively asked, "What the fuck do you think you are doing, that could be my husband for all you know!" I had unfortunately dealt with the wrong person that time, which got me a punch in the nose, and left me bloodied and bruised on the floor. Of course, I knew I didn't deserve to be hit by a violent girl in a nightclub, but it was me not believing in myself or calmly considering to myself that David might have just been interested in me rather than her which never entered my mind. As I opened my eyes, there stood random people peering over me like I was a new form of species that had landed on earth. David was leaning right over with his hand out to help me up. I was shaken and scared but mainly embarrassed that this could happen on the night I met this person who had also knocked me for six in his own way. My housemate, Louis, grabbed me, knowing I just wanted to leave, and as I squeezed and stumbled through the crowded dance floor. David quickly told me he wanted to see me again, I knew he had my number, but I wasn't expecting to hear from him again.

As life works in mysterious ways, the very next day, I went into town with my housemates. I felt stupid with my bruised nose and cut that sat under my right eye which the guys found amusing. We walked into Boots and there stood behind the makeup counter was the very girl who punched me. When her face saw mine, her expression dropped and her eyes widened. I walked right up to her and calmly asked, "Do you recommend a good concealer to hide a bruise?"

She replied, "Sorry," looking sheepish and explained she was just drunk when she hit me. I marched over to the manager of Boots and made a complaint about the girl who had assaulted me the very night before, I walked out and never entered that Boots again. Superdrug made a lot more money in Bristol after that.

After meeting David on that fateful night, he had messaged asking to see me. I had told the white lie that I already had plans so he couldn't see my war wounds. It was the following Monday after eager messages from David asking me out for dinner that I decided to meet up with him. Still wearing the cut under my eye and the bruise slightly subsiding, I covered them in makeup I looked forward to seeing him again. We decided to start off with a drink at The Walkabout on Corn Street before heading to dinner. In what we planned for our first date, it wasn't necessarily the best date, drinks and dinner was an obvious easy plan. But in how I felt, it was the best date I had ever been on because everything just fit. The immediate connection was undeniable, and the attraction, physically, emotionally and mentally, didn't need to be mentioned. We laughed at our situation of how we met, and what had happened as we sat and drank cocktails on a Monday night. We spent hours that evening getting to know each other, and when he drove me home, it was the same feeling as I felt when I first saw him that night at the bar. I just knew that was it and he would be part of my life.

Inseparable, that's what we were. Within a few days, I had practically moved all my belongings into David's flat. While I still had my room with my roommates, David would surprise me by showing up unexpectedly to take me out or come and watch movies with me. David didn't take to one of my housemates at all, noticing that this guy had a cruel streak in him as he often tried to put me down and belittle me in front of people. I never told David that one night during one of our house parties, the housemate drunkenly slammed his hands around my throat and threatened me. In fact, I never told anyone. I just kept out of his way after that. So, when David came over on a quiet casual Wednesday night to take me to the cinema, David decided to get his own back on this bully. Opening up that roommate's half drank bottle of Jack Daniels, knowing it was his as he was the only person in the house that drank it, I thought David was going to drink it, but instead, David very steadily pissed into the bottle before replacing the lid and shaking it up vigorously. We laughed like naughty schoolchildren as we left the house. Watching any film at the cinema together became impossible because we couldn't keep our hands off each other. We had turned into giddy teenagers, kissing and shouting out loud how much we were in love with each other so people in the street could hear.

With so many fun nights out, we quickly learnt the chemistry between us made our dancing together feel incredible. There was a sexual fire between us and knew it would never go away, we were in love, and we were happy.

After one fancy dress night out for his friend's birthday, where the theme was superheroes, I wanted to be a little different and decided to go as Spiderman. The only problem was, pretty damn drunk and walking home from the fun night, I needed a wee. With no places left open to go in the cubicle, I either had to take my entire spider-suit down in the street exposing my entire naked body, or I had to wee straight through it. I decided to find a quiet spot while David, dressed as He-Man stood and watched out for people. As I peeled down the entire Spider suit, I decided to leave the full head mask on to remain unknown. I was now naked Spider-Girl. I was half way through my long alcoholic wee when two policemen walked by and caught me naked but anonymous. As one of them asked for my name, I pulled up the suit and proudly replied, "I'm Spiderman," in a super hero style voice as though they might actually believe me. It was right there I was given an ASBO, but David and I just laughed so much together. I still have the ASBO to this day even though it only lasted for six months on indecent exposer, public urination and attempting to fool a police officer with my superhero voice.

While I worked at Warehouse clothing store over the Christmas and New Year period, it was only weeks into the relationship. I would receive texts and surprise lunch visits

15

from David that made me smile all day. On my lunch break, I received a message with lyrics to a song he liked and thought I wouldn't know. It was a song called 'Morning Afterglow' by a band from the 90s called Electrasy, and I happened to know and love the song. When he sent me the lyrics and I told him I already knew the song too, he couldn't believe it. From that moment on, 'Morning Afterglow' became 'our song'.

David had met me at a very unfortunate time. I had been living a life that had been dampened by my past and I wasn't even aware of my own issues, let alone started to sort them out. For over ten years, I was carrying around and had submerged myself with resentment, anger, pain and inability to accept my past. Around the same time I met David, I had started some acting work around Bristol, appearing in Channel 4's Skins and Holby City, getting theatre parts and trying out some modelling. I was even offered a decent part in BBC's Casualty and on the morning of filming, I just didn't turn up. There were days I really struggled to get out of bed, and I didn't understand why. I was never open to any opportunity offered to me and I didn't think I deserved it, or that it would amount to anything. It was a whole lot easier to sabotage things myself or just walk away. I had a broken mind; a lost soul and I was unaware that anything was even wrong with me. I was a closed mind to anything positive entering my life, and that included David. I may have fallen in love for the first time and initially felt happy, but a few weeks into the New Year while this amazing person who loved me was showing me a life I wasn't used to, I felt overwhelmed and stifled. I was constantly anxious and paranoid underneath the glossy smile I had on display. I was also wildly defensive towards anyone or anything and I felt like the world was constantly against me. But underneath all the hostility, I was nothing but a soul that longed for love and success, although I didn't believe I deserved either. I often became completely emotionally dependable on anyone that could take me away from the inner turmoil I had pushed to one side for so many years. Yet, I had a way of closing myself off from people too. As soon as someone was close, I started to push them away. A walking contradiction of wanting to be accepted and loved so much, but never letting anything good enter my life properly. It felt easier to push things away first before they had the chance to hurt me.

Throughout my life, I was often seen as this confident, well put together person who had her shit together. And I was always confident in many ways. Stand me in a room full of strangers, and I could go and make some new friends. I had always thought of myself as a simple to read, open book person because I was always very forward and upfront. If I liked someone or something, people knew about it. If I felt an emotion, it was on display. "Be true to yourself, be genuine," my mother told me. Growing up, I was an eccentric. I liked to beat the sound of my own drum, not following the crowd and doing things when I wanted. I grew up living life as the class clown, reading my poetry in front of the class when I was as young as five years old. I would attempt to Opera sing in a comical way whilst standing on the tables in math class. I was eventually voted funniest person in my school year book when I was sixteen and was advised to go into comedy or acting. But my confidence and bold approach to life seemed to confuse people when I went through life apologising, explaining myself, and getting defensive and angry over the smallest of things. People didn't understand how I was looking at life through dim grey tinted glasses that had been placed in front of my eyes for so many years.

As time went by, my grey tinted glasses grew bigger, and darker and heavier, to a point where I was attracting very negative things in my life and losing my grasp of anything positive that came close to me. Unfortunately, cracks began to show very quickly for David. It suddenly hit me that I wasn't used to such love in my life. By 2008, when David and I had been together just over a year, my mind and my life was literally spiralling out of control. Underneath the excited fresh new smiles of the new relationship, I was still overwhelmed. I didn't know how to handle such an immense change in my life. From a life of disappointments and loneliness, to letting someone in and living this new life made me feel uneasy. David never saw me for the broken girl I was when he first met me. There were years of pain I walked with and the burdens I carried on my shoulders with sheer anxiety I held inside my brain. But I still wasn't even aware of these problems. It was as though my conscious ability to understand my own problems were covered in repeated layers of paper mache, desperately trying to crack open and wash away.

Four years before I even knew David existed, I started my degree in drama and creative writing at university in Worcester. I was excited to get away from the small town of Cheltenham where I grew up and be physically away from the upbringing I had. I studied drama and creative writing, and like everyone else, I was caught up in the lifestyle where drinking every night was accepted and I never knew how damaging this was to my mental health. I often found myself in very negative situations of aggression and hostility when I was so drunk on endless nights that eventually merged into one. Drinking became a part of my life and even though I didn't like who I was while I was doing it, I kept on going. Underneath all the shenanigans of drinking and partying, and even all the fun my friends and I were having, university turned into a hazy cloud that dominated the next three years and gave me no time to reflect on anything.

Sex and drugs never interested me during my time at university. My father, a heroin addict, who forced me to witness some of the most frightening and unimaginable things a child should encounter. And my mother who had me at 18 and sent me through a roller coaster ride of unpredictable and uncertain times throughout my childhood before she threw me onto the streets at sixteen. This made both sex and drugs off limits in my life. Thoughts of taking any drugs or having sex panicked me as I was convinced if I did either, I would turn out like my parents. So, I consciously chose to go down the opposite road. But for a loud and proud 21-year-old virgin, I quickly earned the nickname 'Cock Tease' amongst the boys at university. My revealing outfits of pink frills that covered nothing and sequined trousers with splits daringly cut to the very top of the leg, along with my flamboyant and outgoing nature often had the boys place bets who could 'fuck me first' rather than just ask me out on a date. I felt even worse when I heard that guys didn't even believe I was still a virgin. As much as I enjoyed a flirt and a snog, I just wanted to save my virginity for someone special and experience a relationship. I may have danced on stages and podiums; I may have drunkenly spun my top around my head before flinging them into the crowds then have to ask random guys to borrow their t-shirt to wear going home. I was the loud, brash, ballsy one of our girl group, but I questioned why people wouldn't believe under the tenacious show girl, I was just a person that didn't feel the need to do all the things I was told I had to try and do at university. I found myself getting wound up, and worked up wondering and festering for hours on end why people would think I would lie about my virginity instead of just having the self-worth and acceptance to say 'that's OK if you don't believe'. Why did it even matter to anyone if I was a virgin or not anyway, regardless of my age, dress sense and outrageous dance moves?

The amount of alcohol I drank, of course took its toll on me and during my second year of university, one fateful night of drinking too much and accepting shots from strangers, was a night that left me disturbed and distressed for a long time. I woke up on a cold winter's morning of 2004 in bed, to discover my body covered in blood. With no memory, no pain, no idea what to think, I went to my friend's bedroom who I had been out with the night before, to find her fast asleep. As I woke her up, her face turned frightened as she looked down at my crotch, to see the blood that surrounded it. I went straight to the doctors and the police. At the doctors, I was tested for any drugs that could still be in my system which, two days later, results showed negative. The worst part was being examined internally whilst two female police officers sat behind a screen. I looked at the outline of their reflection through the thin white sheet that hung between us. Pain soared through my body as the doctor looked inside me as I lay with my legs open, trembling and vulnerable. I was then informed that I had a three-inch cut inside my vagina, and he suspected that this person had inserted something inside me while I was unconscious. I didn't know what to say. It didn't quite compute in my thoughts that this could have happened to me. Police took my bloodied clothes and took photos of finger shaped bruises that surrounded my arms. I was questioned, I gave a statement and all the while I wondered why I was doing this. I couldn't remember a thing. I just wanted it all to go away. I wanted to know if I was still a virgin. I hadn't saved it and waited that long just to be told I had lost it to some random stranger or worse still, had been raped. But as I asked the police their thoughts on the matter, I remember the female police officer asking why I used tampons if I was so fixated on my virginity. I was dumbfounded that I was asked such a bizarre question. I never once cried about what had happened that night and I never had any flashback or memory to it. No one was caught, no one knew anything, and waking up in my bed alone was the strangest mystery of it all.

Despite what had happened, and with the aggressive, defensive and unpredictable behaviour I had dished out, I also laughed a hell of a lot. I also learnt a lot, and made good friends, who knew me well and trusted I was a fun, genuine person who just had a lot of issues, but didn't we all? I enjoyed the freedom university gave me to express myself and get away from my chaotic dysfunctional family in Cheltenham. I soon realised that those were the years I would only experience once in my life. I would never be able to chase that dragon again so I'm glad I got those times and memories.

So, four years later, on that mild January day in 2009, enough was enough. I had pushed that self-destruction button one too many times. Mine and David's relationship had been an exciting, intoxicating and passionate adventure, with an intense love for one another. But my darker side, which I hadn't faced up to or dealt with, spilt out over and over and over again. I had been breaking down, testing and tarnishing an incredible relationship with my insecurities, paranoia, possessive and irrational behaviour. I was always hitting that sabotage button whenever something good came along in my life because I was trapped in a cycle where this was the easy option. It became my defence mechanism. If I pushed someone or something away first, I wouldn't have to deal with being let go, not needed, not desired any longer. David had been trying to make it work for months, but my harmful, complicated mind had pushed David over the edge and ultimately pushed him away. After all that time around me, having to see me every day filled with anger, bitterness, resentment, a negative mind and a closed heart, David needed breathing space. We had spoken about my past and the pain I was still holding on to, but David's hands were tied. Too many years had gone by with me lashing out, starting fights, flying off the handle, and thinking the world was against me. I still wasn't remotely aware, or ready to admit I had some serious issues, and things were about to get a whole lot worse.

I was devastated and felt an overwhelming sense of fear, anticipating what life would be without him. Thoughts of losing him completely filled me with dread but those feelings were cushioned by the fact that we decided to just have some time out and give each other some freedom and alone time to work out what we wanted and live our own lives. I knew deep down it wasn't over, but what I wasn't aware of, was for how long we were to be apart, and what I would need to experience and go through, before getting back together. We needed that time to think if we could be together. Or in fact, if he could be with me. But most importantly, I needed this to happen, for me to realise and reflect on how I was as a person. I needed help and I wasn't ready to admit that yet. As I had packed up my things ready to leave, David held me as we said goodbye, he rubbed my arms and whispered to me, "I don't think this is the end..."

Caroline and Nathan, two friends who had been living at Thorsby House on Church Street for over a year. From the first moment I moved in, there was a sense of feeling unwelcome. I arrived with my bags not to be greeted, not to be spoken to and no offer of helping me with my things up the three flights of stairs. It wasn't a great start. As I piled up all the things I ever owned in my life into the single bed box room, I felt an overwhelming sense of loneliness. Caroline appeared to be a busy, on the go career girl, often on nights out so I never really got the chance to get to know her. Nathan, whom I found especially cold and calculated, often spoke to me like I was beneath him. Two days after moving in, they went to the pub after dinner and didn't invite me along. I sobbed into my pillow as I missed the warmth of David beside me.

A few days later, David had come over to put some shelves up for me in my bedroom and we spent a little time together, but I sensed he was keeping some distance. I was struggling to understand and accept the changes and never considered that time apart could be a positive thing.

As the weeks went by, I was beginning to feel more and more isolated. David was thinking to move out of our flat to save money and meet new people, and I was seeing less of him.

My sadness was filling me up, growing bigger and deeper. I didn't really know anyone in London apart from the people I was working with as a receptionist and I didn't have the money to start a class or do anything fun in my spare time. Above all, I missed David more than ever and the love I had was never going to go away.

Whenever I spent a large amount of time alone, or let my mind wonder, I often wrote poetry. I must have been five or six years old, when I first wrote a poem which was called My Family. I read it out in front of English class, and it was then my teacher, Mr Thomas, asked me to write some more. My second poem was called Ian Theophilus, about a boy I fancied. So, I read it out to the class the following week. Ian sat there, red-faced, while the rest of the class enjoyed listening to the rhyming words of this boy I fancied so much. Over the years, I felt writing poetry released a lot of pain and frustration for, and whether it was a comedy poem or not, it was a way of expressing myself in a positive way.

One Friday night alone in the flat, I sat on my bed and looked around my little box bedroom when I wrote a poem about Caroline and Nathan. It was my way of trying to turn my sad situation into comic words that might make me smile.

The previous night, Caroline had a one-night stand. She and the random man in question were fucking so hard it made the pictures on my wall fall off and smash. Plus, it only reminded me I wouldn't be getting any action for some time myself. But once the shagging had stopped, the random bloke suddenly walked into my room, stark bollock naked thinking it was the bathroom. To add insult to injury, he then asked me if I cared to join them; he didn't even bother to introduce himself! As I asked him to vacate my room, I was a little shaken, considering it was dark in my room and all I could see was an over grown bush of black pubic hair, surrounding a semi erect penis.

Nathan, being the unpleasant person that he was, on several occasions had completely patronised me when he spoke at me. And one day that same week, he had decided that the kitchen was 'his area' and I wasn't to step into it until he was out of it.

So, I wrote the poem. A poem to let out my frustration and make a shitty time laughable. It was my only way at the time to handle those moments.

Tweedle Dee and Tweedle Twat

If I'd have known what I was letting myself in for, I'd have begged a smelly homeless man to be my lodger.

Instead, I moved in with Nathan, a pro cyclist who wore lyre shorts to show off his tiny todger.

Then there was Caroline. They weren't a couple, just an odd, opposite pair.

Him with his skinny frail body and balding head, her with an Amazonian frame covered in hair.

Nathan's voice cut through me like a blunt knife—his monotone Pittsburgh accent was so frightfully dull;

Caroline's not quite as bad, but I should have known what she'd be like... Coming from a place like Hull.

Friday nights, Nathan spent boiling, frying, grating, grilling, chopping, stirring, baking.

Caroline spent fucking, banging, stripping, sweating, panting, squealing... and clearly, faking.

I thought Nathan was gay, as he only brought home men of a certain class.

So I listened intently against my wall, through the thin-rimmed glass.

Turned out, he was an asexual; there was never a peep or tug of a wank.

Caroline was the opposite; I was kept awake by the sound of her receiving a spank.

Mornings were a nightmare, I always got the shower last and the soap would be covered in pubes.

Caroline always got in there first, using all the hot water to scrub the stale cum from her boobs.

Every night, I'd sit in my room alone cuz Nathan would flick through the TV, rocking in his rocking chair.

When he moved out, I played darts with that seat, turns out I have quite a flair.

It was all like an episode from 'The Young Ones' (without the friendship of Vivian, Neil and Rick).

So don't live with strangers, live with friends, or you could end up with a nymph and a sour dick.

People who know me know that money, people with lots of money, celebrities, businessmen, and anything in the world of expensive possessions and wealth didn't really impress me or faze me. Anyone I met, anyone who talked about their wealth made me cringe. Hard work or a talent was what attracted me to people, and some of the most talented people I were to meet in London didn't have two pennies to rub together, but they had soul.

When I got my first job in London working for Rolex head office in Mayfair, it was no big deal. I just needed a job. The place would bring in the rich and famous who came to get their watches serviced, fixed and cleaned.

While I worked at Rolex, I was given one of their watches that I had to wear during the day; I found it bulky and heavy as it swivelled around my wrist all day. As soon as my shift was over, I never left the building with it. I didn't want to be seen with it on. I had already been pigeon holed at work when I joined that I was a spoilt rich daddy's girl just because I made myself presentable, so the last thing I wanted was to be seen in public wearing a Rolex watch,

I felt I had to explain myself to the people at work who presumed things about me and my life, instead of having the self-worth to not care if they thought I was something I wasn't. But this was six years before I started therapy, so I didn't have a clue then.

The singer Simon Le Bon was a regular customer who came into the head office. He was a very pleasant, polite man who spoke to me like a normal human being. Ironically, it was the people that didn't have the fame but had the wealth who came in who spoke to me and the other girls like dirt. I never quite understood just because they had some money in the bank, why they thought they were so high and mighty. Often, they would march straight through the large double doors, no hello but a demand barked at us. One customer had bought their Rolex abroad and came in snarling at me that his watch didn't

24

work while waving it in front of my face. I sometimes had to give the breaking the news that the watch, in fact, was a fake. I couldn't help but feel just a little smug inside. Karma sprung to mind that day.

Once I had settled in a little, I made two friends I would spend time with outside of work. The occasional night out and a Saturday lunches here and there helped take the edge off a lonely time. Valentine's Day had come, and I received a surprise bunch of a dozen red roses, which made me smile because I knew they could only be from one person. David and I were in contact some days over text but living apart was extremely difficult for me. I spent most days at work emailing David lyrics to songs and poems I had written, as my way of telling him how lost I felt without him. I had never felt anything like this before and I didn't know what to do with myself. I felt my heart breaking every day and I was riddled with guilt for how badly I had messed up our relationship.

Before I knew it, March had arrived, with David breaking the news that he was moving out of our flat that we rented together. He was going to be living with two girls and one guy, and my reaction wasn't rational. I panicked, I cried, I went into a state of frenzy imagining all the things that would happen and how I would lose him forever. Feeling overwhelmed and living my days letting my vivid scenarios take over took my thoughts were a nightmare to control. I was a victim of my own mind and I didn't know how to be free.

Within days of David moving in to his new place, he became Facebook friends with his three new housemates, and I got to check them out immediately. To someone on the outside, I would have looked nothing more than a crazy ex-girlfriend stalking these strangers, but to me, I wasn't an ex, I was someone who he still loved, and I loved him back. And when I really listened to my gut, I knew deep down we would get back together, I just didn't know when.

I had only just joined Facebook myself so getting home and with my second-hand laptop that had the letter 'S' missing, I looked intently at the first girl, Clair. She clearly had a boyfriend and looked extremely young. A sigh of relief filled my body. One down, one to go. The other girl, Laura had a completely open Facebook page for anyone to see. She was a normal looking single girl-next-door type and seemed to have a huge interest in baking. I felt more relief she was definitely not David's type. My over-imaginative mind was put to rest. But not for long.

David and I were still in contact, but as the weeks went by, I first felt something was wrong when David never invited me to his new flat. He was really starting to back away from me and wasn't in contact as much. I was occasionally checking Laura's Facebook page and felt a stab of dread when I saw David had written on her wall a few times. One post, about them making a blueberry pie together, twisted my insides and made me sick with jealousy. I had often asked David why I was never invited over to his, considering we still went out for drinks and dinner. But I felt David was slipping through my fingers and the more I tried to hold on, the more he turned into sand. With my stomach tied in knots, I knew my gut was telling me something wasn't right, but I didn't want to admit the truth. The thought of hearing those words 'I have met somebody else' would tear open my heart.

It was the beginning of April and that spring of 2009 was a lot warmer than previous years. I hadn't heard from David in days and my mind was going into overdrive. I was constantly texting him, obsessing and feeling like I was going crazy. People around me at Rolex didn't know what to do with me as I was either crying, raging with anger or a combination of the two. I was totally lost and drowning in despair. I found myself checking Laura's Facebook page daily. I sat, and analysed her latest updates and photos, checking to see if there were any hidden meaning behind the words that could somehow be linked to David. It had become an obsession that was progressively taking over my life. And on the Sunday morning of April 12th, I had once again looked up Laura's page and, to my horror, saw that she had taken David to a friend's garden party, where they were in fancy dress. I felt a stab of hate towards them, as I gazed across the smiling photos of them having fun together. He was dressed as Fred Flintstone, and she was dressed as what was either Dorothy from *The Wizard of Oz* or *Alice in Wonderland*. I couldn't really figure it out. I was now obsessed, intertwined with every detail I could find about her and about their growing relationship. Twisting myself in knots and using all my energy to investigate their every move, I was exhausted from my spying. It had eaten up my time and swallowed up any positive hope I had left for me and David to reunite again.

I had spent weeks crying, seething, sitting in my room, wallowing, getting myself worked up into such a frenzy. I was making myself sick with all the crazy assumptions as I felt my heart breaking more and more. I remember telling myself, if I found out they were a couple, I would track her down and tear her face off. It turned out the reality is never quite what we imagine it to be.

Then there it was, May 16, the photo that is still as clear to me now as the moment I first saw it; Laura's profile picture of her and David kissing.

When I think about the pain I felt when I lost David to Laura, words can't really comprehend the state I fell into. An overwhelming sense of loss and hopelessness to the point of being sick. My body literally went into shock. Deep numbness spread over me when I always thought anger would take over. The reality was entirely different to the imaginary.

I felt like everything was meaningless without David. I remember staring at the photo for at least four hours. Piecing the parts of the picture together in my brain. Making sure it really was him in the photo, burning the image into my brain so it never left. My body felt like it couldn't function. I couldn't even think clearly. I was consumed in a strange sense of pain. Heartache. My heart literally did ache.

Countless movies, entire books and endless poems have been created that revolved around the feeling of a broken heart. Even though I knew there were people out there feeling that same empty heavy heart as I was, it could never console me. Nothing could prepare me for what I was going to feel. Nothing could make me feel better. No one could make me smile. A sinking, dark cloud filled me up with the pain that ate up my insides and it felt like I was drowning.

After staring at the photo, using up every grain of energy I had, I eventually fell into a deep, exhausted sleep. Waking up with the initial thought that it had been nothing but a terrible dream, I was once again covered with all the dark feelings that surrounded me; sadness and grief.

Over the next few weeks, there were days when I woke up that I wished I hadn't. The sinking heart wrenching, stomach churning, sickening feeling inside of me. After I had seen that photo, I didn't contact David. And David had stopped contacting me. A blur of timeless empty space filled up those weeks in 2009 when it all felt like one long day that would never end. However, I remember taking a moment and listening to my intuition. What was my heart telling me? And right there was one grain of hope that somehow managed to get inside me. And that was, I knew they wouldn't last. I knew Laura, as opposite to me as she was, was right for David just in that time in his life after dealing with the chaos and unstable life that I could only offer him. But I knew he still loved me. I just had to wait and live with the pain until we were both in the right time of our lives to come back together again. I held on to this and never let go.

Whenever I wrote a poem in a short amount of time, I often asked myself if it was written correctly and doubted if I was any good. But they were true feelings laid out on paper. Two days after seeing that photo, I wrote a poem, it was the only way I could express the pain that I felt.

Ironic

The last drop of hope was snatched from my heart,
I don't know how to accept that we are officially apart.

The words I read, cut through me so cold,
I dreaded to know the truth I knew would be told.

My images that once filled my mind are no longer just thoughts,
cuz what happened was real, your lies I never bought.

My black hole now deepened with each lie that comes true,
she was always so close, that much I just knew.

My sweetness turned sour, my bitterness so strong,
cuz with all of our bad times, I still thought I would
belong.

This nightmare that haunts me and taunts me my pain,
I know in my life I'll never love this way again.

You never told me straight if she was just a friend,
but if love has grown there, don't tell me, for I'll never
quite mend.

My heart is now frozen, no one can come close,
for my heart is now broken, other people's love is no
dose.

The strongest of arms can't keep me from harm,
the sweetest of man can't make me feel calm.

For I am alone, and my soul is now steel,
I don't even know where to begin this long lonesome
heal.

Your love words mean nothing, from the actions you
chose,
I can now see so clearly past the end of my nose.
It's ironic that I write this, with your choices so raw,
my pain is how yours was, but I've learnt from before.

I don't know why I sent this, and if you love me no
more.
These words will mean nothing, like an ex you had
before.

I pray to the star you gave, that you don't want to
replace,
and when you see your strong future, you still see my
face.

I was handling David and Laura being together so sorely
and bitterly, it consumed my day-to-day living. The emphasis

of not caring about anything, including myself, took its toll. From the beginning of 2009, my life started to unravel. I would be at work saying hello to customers, with tears rolling down my face. I would spend every spare moment fantasising about being back with David or wondering what plans he was making with her. And worst of all, my inner demons had been set free. My self-destruct button had been pushed. I didn't care about myself anymore so why would I care about anything else.

I always believed if you are thinking and feeling a certain way, you attract certain things. When my inner resentment, bitterness, anger and my unacceptance emerged, trouble entered my life. On July 10th, 2009 two things happened. Rolex had enough of the unpredictable moods I bought into work for the last four months, therefore, on that summer's day, I was fired. I remember almost floating out of the grand building, feeling as though I was nothing more than a vast empty void that had nowhere to go. I felt mislaid as the company I had worked at for fourteen months had just let me go that way. This was only the second time in my life I had been fired. I was scared what to do next and how I was going to pay my rent suddenly really frightened me.

But on that very same day, less than eight hours later, I received a text message from David for the first time in months. My heart skipped a beat and pounded twice as fast as I opened the message to reveal he was thinking of me and missed me. I couldn't believe it. But I knew he was still with Laura and the small grain of delight I may have felt was diluted by the mourning I was feeling that day from being fired. I knew I had to find a new job and fast. The recession was at its worst in years, so I knew that I wasn't going to find a job as easy as the previous year. But I had to be determined. I had no choice.

Living in the large capital city for less than eighteen months alone with no job was daunting. I literally knew nothing about the locations of where the job agencies were across London. I was a lost little girl. I had found Rolex by walking into a recruitment agency on the off chance, so this was all I knew. I had never heard of websites like 'Secs in the city' or 'Monster' to find jobs sitting at home where you could send agencies your CV with a click of a button. So, after being fired from Rolex, I spent the next three weeks walking across

London and back, handing in my CV personally to all the job agencies by hand, one by one.

July 2009 was one of the hottest summers for years, and with its recession, three weeks out of work and not even a sniff of an interview I was beginning to panic. But with no job, and no money, I had no food. And the money I had left in my account was for August's monthly rent. The stress of looking for a job plus the sweltering heat blasted away my appetite. With my adult life being 10 stone wearing size 10 clothes, I was losing weight fast. And not intentionally.

Not being in work, having no contact with David and walking around London looking for a job quickly had a knock-on effect on my body which I didn't even notice at first. One morning, with a hand full of spare CVs, I pulled on a t-shirt and a denim skirt, and made my way towards Embankment where there was a cluster of recruitment agencies. Just as I walked across the busy main road that met Big Ben, my skirt fell to my ankles. A car stopped and beeped whilst a young man dressed in a builder's uniform with his high vis jacket and dusty trousers shouted across the street 'Oi Oi!' to me. I couldn't believe it. I had been out of work for a month and I had lost a stone in weight. With my 5'9 height, I had plummeted to under 9 stone. When I went home and let my skirt fall off me again, I looked at myself in the mirror and saw someone I didn't recognise. My bones were protruding, my eyes had sunk, and my sadness deepened as I wept alone in my room.

It was then I turned to the one thing that made me escape the reality and feed my body, shoplifting. Like someone turning to drink or drugs, this was something inside my brain where I never really registered the actions or decisions I made doing it, I just turned to it. The same as if someone turned to eat excessive amounts of food or gambled away all their money. It was that deep-rooted resolution that temporarily filled a void and made me feel good for a few moments. I never really comprehended or reflected on this action that I turned to, I knew that it was illegal, immoral and dishonest but those reasons not to do it never entered my head. They don't when you are desperate and unhappy. I knew that hours after doing it, I felt bad about myself. But all I knew at the time was it felt so good and it was my own sorry escape to the reality of how low I was in life.

The first time I ever shoplifted, I was 13 and I didn't stop until I was 17. This was the only other time in my life where for some unknown reason, I turned to shoplifting rather than anything else that made me feel better about myself. My step-dad had been part of my life for two years, and had been mentally, emotionally and verbally abusing me. At twelve years old when I was starting puberty, he would measure my bath water before I got in to make sure the water didn't cover my body. He would often beat me with a wooden spoon while forcing me to hold on the back on a chair. The bedroom I slept in when we moved in with him had half the wall missing, and with no hoover, I had to sweep up the rubble and dust that fell from the fallen brickwork each day. A daily dose of him calling me a slut and a cunt entered my ears too as he walked past me, and made sure my mother didn't hear. The worst part was his parents who never accepted me because I wasn't Bills child. Going to their house for Sunday lunch was something I dreaded. Bill's mum wouldn't acknowledge me and would talk to me as though I didn't belong there. This was a disturbing change from the few years I had been living alone with my mum after she threw my father out for taking heroin on a daily basis in front of me. Shoplifting when I was thirteen was my escape, my mental sanctuary. I would get a thrill from the adrenalin and feel happy for a while with the goods that I managed to get away with. It was usually makeup from Boots that I would lay on my bedroom floor and just gaze upon it for a while. I usually gave the makeup away to friends at school or just collected it up and never used it.

When Bill threw me out on to the streets, with no help from my mother to keep me, I had just turned sixteen. I didn't talk to my mum for three years after that day. The resentment I held for her letting that happen to me consumed me. But once Bill was out of my life, the shoplifting eventually died down. I just had no idea of the impact it had on my mental health for years to come.

I didn't shoplift again until the summer of 2009 when I was 26. I just never realised it was something that could became part of me and my life for so long once I started again. An activity that slowly took over me like a drug. Shoplifting WAS my drug and I thought I was in control of it. Before I knew it, it was controlling me and my day-to-day life. Not getting caught was also a danger, I felt untouchable, in control, powerful and momentarily happy. It began that summer with simply needing to eat. I had no money to my name, and it was easy to steal food. Taking a packet of crisps and eating them in the shop, grabbing a sandwich and taking it to the shop's toilet, and quickly scoffing it down there. But like any addiction, that feeling soon wore off, and I needed something bigger and better to fill me. Literally.

I was starting to feel paranoid every time I ate food in the shops, assuming people would find me with empty wrappers and containers. Then came up with the idea of stealing items that I could eat outside of the shops. Items that were easy to conceal. Items worth stealing that I knew would fill me up for the next few hours. And then I thought, smoked salmon. Flat, filling and with its fatty acids, I wanted to gain some of the weight I had lost. I often flicked through the magazines in Marks and Spencer's on my lunch breaks in the past instead of buying them, I would breath in the glossy fashion pages before placing them back, looking spotless and untouched. So, picking up Vogue magazine, I carried it around the food market of M&S on Oxford Street. I picked up a £10 packet of Scottish smoked salmon and slipped it into the magazine, as though it were a free sample for people to try. I thought this was a master plan of an idea. I would then walk out, holding my stolen issue of Vogue magazine under my arm, the way business people held their Daily Telegraph on their way to the office. I suddenly had a flash back to the times I shoplifted all those years ago when I was so desperately unhappy by the hands of my mother's husband, and the feeling I got when I was eventually caught when I was a scruffy 13-year-old. But as a grown up, looking polished and well kept, I assumed I wouldn't be what society may think a typical shoplifter 'should' look like. Appearances can be deceiving, I looked like a relatively well-off girl with her hair and makeup in the right place who could hold herself in a way no one would ever suspect. Who would have thought this girl had no money, no job and was shoplifting large amounts of expensive fish? And remarkably, I was getting away with my smoked salmon magazine plan. I would go in once a day after handing in more CVs, feeling physically and mentally drained of walking so far, and being repeatedly asked why I 'wanted to be a receptionist' when I didn't. My smoked salmon lunch activity would wake me up again and fuel me with the adrenalin I needed. Three weeks went by, and I had stolen so many issues of Vogue and other magazines, I started to leave them in coffee shops and public toilets, fanned out for women to read. I may have gone a little loopy and possibly overdosed on smoked salmon.

As well as feeling continuously hungry, I was also feeling extremely lonely. I made the bad but desperate decision to accept a date from a man who asked me out in the street. A rich businessman who I didn't find remotely attractive, with his combed back hair smothered in gel and his smug grin. He had approached me and insisted I take his number as he wanted to take me out to dinner. I found him arrogant and a little creepy. But as I looked inside my empty refrigerator, seeing no food of my own, I messaged the guy and reluctantly accepted the dinner. On the date, he took me to a fancy restaurant in Chelsea and within minutes, I knew not only did we have nothing in common, we lived very different lives and I felt no chemistry with this chauvinistic person. To strangers on the outside, we looked like two people out on the town in, eating expensive steak. But on the inside, I was broken. I had prostituted myself for a free meal. Every bite may have been filling me up, but it also made me feel more and more empty. Towards the end of the meal, he suggested going back to his place for a threesome with a girl 'he knew' that could come around on demand. I felt I had reached one of my lowest points as I sat in the chair opposite this person. I felt sick inside. And with every bite of my meal became harder to swallow, I excused myself quickly and politely left, telling him I wasn't interested in that. From him having my number, I had to eventually block his harassing messages asking for drinks out and sex at his apartment. I felt I had lost a lot of self-respect over the last few weeks, but I kept what remaining dignity I had and was proud to walk out of the restaurant with my head held high without him.

I wasn't proud, but like any addiction, it grew. The shoplifting soon hit another level when I could get away with eating full lunches in cafes and restaurants, walking away holding a piece of paper that looked like a card machine receipt. Busy places were easy when waitresses were rushing around but I left feeling sick with guilt. Cafes in supermarkets and departments stores were the easiest to get away with, as I could easily walk around the shop for a while or sit in the corner without being noticed. I needed food, I still hadn't found a job, I had no money left and I was managing to block out any feeling of what I was doing on a daily basis. On some level, there was my conscience telling me what I was doing was wrong because I knew never to steal from family businesses or individual people. The thought of taking from a person or private business was out of the question. But the reality was, I was still breaking the law and I never once registered how far it was going to go.

Each day that went by, handing out my CV, registering to job agencies but with no call coming my way, stealing food was nothing more than an everyday task. Moving onto other things was inevitable, I needed a bigger fix to feed the habit. Clothes, makeup, shoes, bags, perfume, beauty products, costume jewellery anything I could get my hands on to fill the void. I even found myself walking to Topshop which, at the time, sold packets of full heads of hair extensions. I would literally take them out of the box and put them in my hair inside the shop, and walk out wearing them all shiny and new. I would often go home with bags full of stolen items that I didn't want or need. Once I got home, I would lay everything down on my floor and gaze upon my work, calculating how much I had stolen and what it was all worth. For a moment, I felt I had accomplished something. These items looking up at me gave me some sense of comfort. But once that warm feeling had faded, I was left empty again. Swamped with guilt thinking about the person I had become, I often gave away the items to charity and sometimes even took them back to the shop, placing them where I had found them.

On a particularly frustrating day, filled with anger and the feeling that I was losing control, I stole a £200 bag with the alarm tag still on it. I didn't even want it and I KNEW the alarm tag was still on it. But I didn't care. Maybe on some level I wanted to get caught. As the store alarms went whirling off in a busy large department store, I just walked out with the bag on my shoulder, cool and calm, as though it must have been someone else causing all the noise and mayhem. As I got far enough away, I wondered how I was going to get this black metal tag off, that only the proper equipment would work. I made the bizarre decision to walk into a Starbucks just off Oxford Street and asked for a pair of scissors. I sat down and cut the metal wire. It set the alarm screaming inside the small coffee shop, leaving everyone looking at me.

"It's just my rape alarm," I announced to the room, handing back the scissors and briskly leaving. All I could do at that point was put the metal tag in the bin, leaving it beeping veraciously with people stopping to look inside. My adrenalin rush and self-fulfilment were getting out of hand.

I knew shoplifting was morally, legally and psychologically wrong, I thanked my lucky stars that whatever it was in my brain that turned me to shoplifting, hadn't turned me to drink, drugs or anything physically harmful to me or anyone else. Shoplifting created a rush of adrenalin, which was my fuel that was now controlling me. It was its own messed up drug. The temporary happiness it gave my spirits was the addictive element to it all. I justified my actions because I had no money and I hadn't given myself a chance to reflect on why I had even gotten into this mess in the first place. Money may have been a part of it, but it was deeper than that, which I hadn't addressed. All I knew, after years of doing it, I was never left with peace of mind. It only made me feel worse. It was an addiction that may have released an intense rush of happiness, but it didn't last very long, it wasn't real. I was seeking the short-term quick fix repeatedly, not understanding the consequences it had on me.

It was coming toward the end of summer when I hadn't answered any calls from any family member or friends I knew before my move to London. I hadn't seen the two girls from Rolex in ages and one Saturday afternoon, sitting across the road from my flat in Clissold Park, feeling desperate and alone, I received a call out of the blue from my grandma. I decided to answer as I lay in the sun. She was asking how I was and checking in on me worried as no one had heard from me for so long. The memory of the conversation with my grandma is blurred and hanging up the phone after what was just a brief, vague conversation because I was not interested in communicating with anyone. All I did after that call was sob into the dry green ground I laid on, praying that this feeling would end, and the situation I had gotten myself into would just stop and for things to be good again. I wanted to see some light at the end of this long bleak tunnel I was stuck in. I had never felt so alone, so desperate and so ashamed of myself with who I was. What was I was doing and where was I going in life? All I wanted was David to hold me tight and tell me everything was going to be OK. I was either a ticking time bomb or a stuck in a bleak dark tunnel. I was either shoplifting, getting myself into fights with strangers on the tube or in the street. I just didn't care and anyone who got in my way, gave me the chance to unleash the pain and anger I was holding. But there were days when I just couldn't even get out of bed. I wouldn't eat for days, and slept in a pair of tights for nights on end just wanting to stay asleep and keep out of the world. There was only one thing left that could keep me from not losing it all together; a course I was about to start that I had forgotten I had enrolled on while I worked at Rolex. A course in stand-up comedy.

October 29th was the date I started a course in writing stand-up comedy. This had been the perfect timing considering how I had been feeling for so long. This course was to stop me falling any deeper in the hole I was already stuck in. Ten weeks of experiencing a brand-new lease of life, meeting new people that mapped out the start of a journey in the field of comedy and entertainment. This was a time in my life that changed everything for the better in many ways. Starting comedy, and finding that new focus gave me the strength to feel inspired and work towards something worthwhile in my life. I may have still had all the financial, emotional and mental issues in my life, but a new chapter was about to begin.

Stand-up comedy was something I never planned to do in life. Writing short stories and poetry was the creative fun I got up to as a child. Then growing up and experiencing acting during my GCSE's, I realised I loved performing. Something about being in front of a live audience was compelling and pretty magical. So, I decided to study Drama and Creative

Writing at Worcester University. It was my university lecturer, David Broster, who suggested I try stand-up comedy. This always stuck in the back of my mind, and I knew I had a gift for comic timing and clowning. I was voted funniest person in school for my eccentric mannerisms, impressions of Cilla Black and how I was never afraid to make a fool of myself, but it wasn't until almost two years of living in London, and a long ten years after leaving university, I made the decision to take it further. Writing was always a massive passion, so this course was perfect. To pass the course, everyone had to perform the comedy they had written and what was to come for me over the next few years, was something I never had anticipated.

I had enrolled for the Camden Comedy Course in early 2009 while I was still working a full-time job at Rolex. I genuinely didn't think about it again from the time I paid the £295 for the ten-week course, until the first day it began on a warm Thursday evening in October.

Turning up, I remember the building feeling like a stuffy old church, with steep narrow stone stairs and paint peeling from the walls. I didn't know what to expect so I tried not having any expectations. I just felt happy I had something to focus on. It was almost as though those months back when I booked the course, I knew I needed something to look forward to and channel myself, and the course turned out to be a new kind of escape from reality for me. A bubble I entered once a week, where I could laugh and engage with people, be creative with no bad feelings around me. Every Thursday evening, for that hour and a half, I felt good again. It was my little haven that kept me from going over the edge.

People that enter my life who become incredibly important to me are always remembered in my mind like a short show reel when I first met them. I can genuinely say those few that are close to me are very clear in my memory, down to what they first said to me, what they were wearing and the way they made me feel. During my second week of attending the Comedy School, we had the chance to meet up with the second group that was held on a different day of the week. Unfortunately, it was almost everyone from my own group, with just one from the other class. A voluptuous girl of my age with the hair of Princess Jasmin and huge brown eyes that looked so alive. She was wearing a canary yellow top and came up to me with a huge smile asking very excitedly, "Are you Naomi Hefter?"

"Yes, how do you know that?" I replied, smiling back. I would usually feel paranoid when someone I didn't know knew my full name, but in that moment, I was happy to speak to this new girl standing next to me.

"I saw your comment on the Comedy School Facebook page and thought you looked fun, I'm Samar," she said with enthusiasm in her voice.

And with that, we became friends instantly and she would be involved in some very poignant times in my life over the next few years.

During my fourth lesson at the comedy school, the group and myself spent our time experimenting with improvisation, which was a huge passion of mine. I was loving every lesson and discovering more about myself as a performer. After a free glass of soda water in the pub nearby with the rest of the class, I caught the bus home. It was now a frosty cold November night and while the bus was almost empty, I sat on the front row seat to myself. As the bus pulled into Euston, my heart stopped as I saw David board the bus. He looked right at me in complete shock and sat two seats behind me. I never even turned around, I didn't need to. I could almost hear his brain ticking away, wondering what to do. And before I knew it, he came and sat next to me and softly said hello. He put his arm around me, and I could only shrug it off immediately in principle, but I wanted him to hold me right there and then forever. I told him he couldn't touch me as he made his decision on who he wanted to be with. Before I knew it, it was my stop and as I struggled to pull myself up from the seat to leave. I felt surprisingly calm knowing deep down that wasn't going to be the last time we saw each other.

Once the ten weeks of the comedy course was over, the class was ready to perform the piece of stand-up comedy each person had written. A showcase was put on in a huge hall in Camden, where friends and family were invited to turn up. Wishing everyone the best of luck, I sat in the dressing room wearing a sequined black dress I had never felt so nervous in my life as I did then. The moment before I walked on stage to perform stand-up comedy for the first time on December 16, I was telling myself I couldn't go through with it. My legs had turned to jelly yet my entire body felt as though it weighed a ton. My writing and performance teacher, who was also a professional stand-up comedian, right there and then, literally pushed me on to the stage to start my set. My five-minute gig that felt like five seconds went incredibly well. I received the reaction I hadn't anticipated but hoped for, so I was very happy. The adrenalin was still pumping through my body even when everyone had finished performing their piece. It didn't really enter my brain to carry on performing my set in the real world of the comedy circuit in London. But because my gig had gone much better than I thought, I was given a list of open-mic nights where you didn't need to book; you could literally show up, wait your turn and perform in front of strangers. In that moment, I knew I had to experience life as a stand-up comedian gigging around London. I had nothing to lose. I felt excited and naively expected my gig to go as well as my first gig had gone in the comedy school. I had no idea that the next six and a half years would be one hell of a ride.

I had also managed to find myself a temporary Christmas job. Finally, those three months out of work felt like I had been out of work for years. I was going to be paid weekly up until the role finished in February, so I was relieved that money would be coming my way soon. And it was also something that could keep me busy and my mind occupied over the Christmas period. The job I was offered needed no interview, as they needed someone urgently and chose me due to my 'vast knowledge of watches'. Of course, the only knowledge I had of Rolex watches was being able to spot a fake one. The job was held at the watch repair and service in Selfridges on Oxford Street. With the reputation the store has, I immediately imagined that I would need look glamorous and would be placed, posing next to the immaculate watch cabinets that got polished after every customer walked by. This sounded better than the last three months I had traipsing the streets of London.

When I turned up on my first day, I had made an extra special effort to look right for the occasion. With my makeup placed to perfection, I had added some curls to my hair and a pair of fluttery black false lashes to my eyes. As it turned out, I wasn't going to be on the shop floor, but instead put at the back of the department store hidden away from the browsing and buying areas, placed in a room no larger than a disabled toilet cubicle. There inside were four other women waiting to be screamed at by customers with their broken watches. I remember feeling my heart sink as I squeezed myself into the room. I introduced myself and apologised as I had my bum up against one of the ladies there who was elderly. It really didn't help that the second lady, as lovely as she was, reeked of BO. The third lady was a pretty Italian girl, but she could hardly speak English, so she was put in one corner of the 'room' to label and package all the broken watches. And the fourth was the manager, Lisa, a stern middle-aged lady who tried her best to not be in the room when everyone else was in there, as it was all too much for her. Within the first five minutes of my first day, it was too much for me also, I thought I was going to scream. Considering how compact the room was and how all I heard was a queue of customers, shouting through the tiny window of our hidden hut at the back of the shop, demanding their expensive watches to be fixed. I had no choice but to stay there. I was broke.

I was always put in the 'window' area of the box room and left to deal with the queue of angry customers, ready to let off their watch problems to me. Because of the size of the 'room' and how chaotic the days were, we were all constantly stressed out with the environment around us. There was no time to get to know each other, no time to have a conversation, and no time to stop and just take a moment. It was always haywire. I had gone from one extreme to another, but I tried not to complain as I was after all earning some money.

The 'pop star', Mike Skinner, from *The Streets* would come in from time to time, each time presenting a different watch. He always looked at me as though he was waiting for me to recognise him and say something. His smug grin quickly turned to impatient huffing when he would have to wait in the line like everybody else. Of course, I pretended I didn't know who he was, I wasn't prepared to play up and entertain his arrogant demeanour.

I still hadn't gained much of my lost weight as I was still behind in my finances, trying to save any money I made for the rent. I was run down and didn't feel well at all. I knew there was something wrong because I hardly ever drank fluids, I could never even finish a cup of tea, let alone drink the litre bottle of water we are all meant to have each day. But I was suddenly weeing a lot more often. I would literally jump up in the middle of the night, desperate to get to the loo, just making it in time, before my magically full bladder released its fluids. What was strange was that not only was I going for a wee a lot more often than usual, the weeing was strangely taking forever and a day to finish. It would not stop! I went to the doctor's and he put me on a course of antibiotics, and told me I had contracted a UTI, a urinary tract infection. When I picked up my prescription, I had two hours before I needed to be in my shoebox of an office at the back of Selfridges. Time to kill often meant window-shopping. All I wanted to do was try on fabulous clothes I couldn't afford. So, I headed to Topshop and found myself two pairs of faux leather trousers, one pair were so beautiful, with a dark grey, metallic finish painted on them, costing £150 which I could never afford. Taking them into the changing room, I vividly remember I had the smallest Boots bag where I had bought a tuna sandwich and some Fruit Pastels. I had placed it down along with my handbag and began to undress, removing my black jeans, ready to pull on the first pair of shiny new trousers. Once I slid them on, they felt incredibly snug around the crotch, but I thought they looked fabulous. But suddenly the urine infection kicked in; out of the blue, I was desperate for a toilet. I felt utterly hopeless as it started to flood out of my body, soaking through the expensive fabric I managed to pull them off me while the wee was still gushing out; I grabbed the tiny Boots bag chucking the food on the floor, and held the bag under my poor sorry flowing vagina as the wee took over. It was then that it came out so fast and hard, the bag split. It was a nightmare of chaotic, wet mess. I had no choice but to use the second pair Topshop trousers to mop up the wee, as it had begun to trickle under the dressing room doors into the next where I could hear someone changing. Before someone would notice, I used the already wet Topshop trousers to soak up the moving wee under the two changing rooms. When the wee finally stopped gushing, I was literally standing in a shallow pool of piss. The Topshop trousers were soaked and slumped in the corner like a limp corpse, laying on top of the split Boots bag. All I could do was put my own trousers back on and run out that door before a person came in to that sorry state of a changing room. I only wish I could have left an apology note to the poor cleaner who had to have cleared up my infected urine.

2009, a year where I spent so alone. Days where I couldn't face getting out of bed. Endless lonely times sat in despair sobbing over the loss of David and how happy he appeared to be with Laura. A year with no money, shoplifting once again like I had as a teenager and felt even worse about myself now I was a grown up. I didn't want to feel that way anymore. Those feelings were so raw for so long. But I hoped, in some way, to never let those feelings wither away completely. I wanted, one day, a comparison to let me appreciate life. The only problem was I had spent most of my life so unaware about my state of mind. I had been suffering from depression, post-traumatic stress and anxiety, but it wasn't for years ahead when I would finally know that about myself. But from falling into such a dark hole in 2009, I had to find the strength from somewhere and claw myself out of it.

2010

"They're only laughing 'cause they wanna fuck you!"

Whenever I got asked the question "What was your childhood like?" I always felt myself seize up. I was never really sure how to answer and which part of my childhood I was meant to talk about. Every time I thought about my childhood, from the age of around six to the age of ten, I felt quite a sense of nostalgia. It was just me and my mother, and we shared happy memories together. Dancing around our little council flat in Cheltenham listening to Kate Bush and Pink Floyd. We were poor, but I was happy because she had thrown my dad out and I was free from his warped actions even when he wasn't high on heroin. A narcissist whose addiction got so out of hand, he not only sold his own car and his saxophone that he played to get his fix, but he sold all of my mother's belongings too. Luckily, the things my mother eventually told me about him and what he did around me, I couldn't really remember. She told me how he would take my Tiny Tears and Cindy dolls, and draw red tears down their faces, as though they had been crying blood. She told me anytime she went out and left him alone with me, she would come back and he would be passed out on heroin. One occasion, on heroin, he passed out whilst watching The Terminator, leaving me to watch it and suffer nightmares for days. My mother told me stories of when he and his friend would go out 'queer bashing' as he liked to put it. Hearing gruesome stories that he had told people in such a proud and accomplished way made me weary of him.

The memories I did have of him stayed with me until I pushed them so far back, I told myself they were just bad dreams. I remember the times he would set my clothes on fire

44

while I was wearing them, then while I was a light, he would quickly put me out and laugh. He also found it amusing to throw large garden spiders at me, watching me scream and wriggle about as I was so scared where the spider had landed. My worst memory of him, which will haunt me for the rest of my life, was when my mum had bought me a kitten and I named him Mowgli from the Jungle Book. As a kitten and still being litter trained, he did a wee on the carpet while mother was in the shower. My dad grabbed Mowgli like a rag doll and strangled the frightened kitten in front of me. My mother came screaming out of the shower from hearing my harrowing cries. While I stood there, watching my pet's face, with my dad's huge hands around his fragile neck, my mother did her best to pull him away. That moment damaged the love for my dad and was never the same again.

So, when he was finally thrown out, all I remember was my dad packing bags and I didn't feel sad or scared of where he was going. I felt calm watching him leave with all his belongings.

There was a short time it was just me and my mum. A couple of boyfriends came and went, we didn't have any spare money and I saw various babysitters while my mother worked at the local hospital. I remember her sleeping a lot when we were together, so I played with the local kids on our road and I enjoyed my own time drawing or writing poems. My mother wasn't the conventional mother. Every morning, she would roll a joint for breakfast, and one after dinner which always embarrassed me when I had friends over from school. She never taught me how to cook or make my bed or the things my friends seemed to know. But she would always tell me to never lie, not to let people use me and most importantly, be true to myself.

Unfortunately, my memories from being ten and onwards went severely downhill from there. My mother re-married suddenly, out of the blue. Before I knew it, we had moved to the other side of Cheltenham and I had to change schools from where I had been my whole life, to finish my last year elsewhere before secondary school. My mother told me years later this changed my personality severely, from loving life and school to being utterly miserable, unsettled and withdrawn. My life had been uprooted and my mother had married this person I didn't really know anything about. All I knew was his name was Bill. A short, aggressive looking man, with a huge beard that covered most his face, and what remained were two cold dark eyes that always seem to glare.

Within months, my life had changed and what was worse, I had too. For six years, before they threw me onto the streets, I was tormented, and abused mentally, verbally, emotionally and psychologically by Bill. He was an inwardly raging person, a walking passive aggressive unpredictable character with a strangely furious angry expression. The times he walked past me to mutter 'cunt' and 'stupid slut' at me, I wouldn't respond, I just sat there as though I hadn't heard. But underneath, my blood would be boiling and I would be left seething. If I left a light on in any room I walked out of, I would be punished for using up resources. If I made myself some pasta on a Saturday afternoon without asking, I would be grounded for not asking. I was constantly being punished, in very old-fashioned, bizarre ways. Being forced to stay in my bedroom for days and sometimes weeks at a time, being made to write 1,000 lines a day, 'I must not behave in this way'. Over and over again, until it drove me crazy.

I was a typical 12-year-old and went through a tomboy phase where I wanted to wear American style baseball jackets, oversized t-shirts and baggy jeans. But Bill never let me. When I secretly bought a pair of black baggy jeans to wear with the pocket money my mum gave me, Bill found them. So as a punishment, my mum would be left standing in the kitchen, while Bill made me hold on to the back of a chair, wearing only t-shirt and knickers, he repeatedly beat the back of my legs with a wooden spoon, I felt utterly humiliated.

Sadness, resentment and bitterness slowly filled inside my heart. My mother never got involved with how Bill was treating me and every time I told her about it, she refused to get involved or even talk about it with me.

This had quite an effect on me during my years at secondary school; I was troubled and never really understood at the time. I was constantly looking for recognition and acceptance. Always being the clown, I enjoyed making the class laugh, even if it meant me being thrown out of lessons.

But during lunch times, I was a bit of a loner, sometimes spending my breaks sitting in the toilets reading books or thinking about my future. I did have one good friend I met when I was fourteen, Clemency McNamara, who lived a few doors down from me. We would spend hours together using our imaginations to create crazy worlds of our own. We laughed for hours as we told ourselves how crackers we were compared to all the normal people sitting around us in class. Teachers either loved us or loathed us. Some teachers didn't want to give me the time of day, whilst others would spend quality time pushing me to do well and offer me support to improve my work.

When we received our yearbook by the time the school years were finished, I had some lovely comments from teachers writing various things which made me smile. From being entertaining and becoming famous, to reminding me to go for anything I wanted in life and being strong, but it was my art teacher, Mr McClelland, who wrote a line that simply read, "Thank you for being a decent human being." That was one of the nicest things anyone had said to me.

I was sixteen and decided not to stay on to do A-levels but to go to GlosCat collage in Gloucestershire to study for a Diploma in Performing Arts. It felt like the right decision and it took me on a path that would lead me to perform professionally. It was only six months into the course when Bill and my mother threw me onto the streets. I came home one Saturday evening after a day at the local Lido, where Bill had locked the doors and wouldn't let me in. As I continuously knocked hard, my mother eventually came to the door and through the chain, told me Bill had packed my belongings and I wasn't welcome anymore. Apart from me and Bill not getting on, I couldn't understand why this was happening. As I screamed and cried and yelled in the streets, I felt pure fear race through my body. I was 16, and I had no idea what and why was happening, and more importantly, where I was going to go.

As Bill put my packed bags into the streets, I was trying to force my way in, screaming at my mother to come and help me, and hold and tell me this wasn't happening.

The sun had gone down, and I was exhausted from my harrowing cries. A taxi had turned up to take me and my things away. I had never felt so rejected in my life and it felt as though my heart had stopped. As Bill shut the door with my mother inside, I asked the taxi driver to take me to a friend's house who I went to collage with. Her name was Sarah, and I thank my lucky stars, because I stayed there for the next two years until our course was over. The abandonment from my own mother had such an effect on my mental health, it caused me real problems in years to come.

I found stand-up comedy a real roller coaster during the year of 2010. I had been on the circuit less than six months, when I was starting to realise how naive I had been about the world of making strangers laugh. I knew there were more intricacies to the art other than just telling jokes; I knew that it wasn't as simple as getting on stage and 'just being funny', while I told the audience my outrageous stories. There was a persona, a presence of 'who you were' as a comedian. A style of comedy which was to portray who you were to the audience. And with all that, there was timing, delivery, first impressions, appearance, voice, tone of voice, reactions, interactions, adlibs, pauses, likability, relatability, expressions, and of course the essence of writing and structuring the joke itself. I had so much to learn and the only way to do this was through experience. I had to expect and prepare myself to get so many things wrong in order to grow before I delivered a professional piece of work. Having that natural 'funny bone' was always the foundation to be a memorable and successful stand-up which gave me the confidence to get out there. But I had a lot to master in the world of stand up, even to the finest detail of how I walked onto the stage and what I wore. I soon discovered, every person whether to ready to perform stand-up comedy, sing a song or give a corporate speech, gets judged, positively or negatively, even before they have opened their mouth. I had to experiment and find out what kind of comic I was, and I was prepared to be judged every single moment. For the first year of performing stand-up comedy, I was a small fish in the ocean. I quickly learnt how it was important to be liked by the crowd and fellow comics, and I needed to play around with that all-important opening line and what tone of voice I wanted within my set. What persona did I want to portray? An excitable storyteller? Deadpan? Fast paced puns? Political? Angry?

Nervous? Arrogant? Mysterious? Abstract? Character? Physical? There were endless ideas and people's opinions being offered to me from so many angles which made it all very confusing. One person told me to use my looks and play on them. Another person was telling me to not bring up my looks, as it would make me appear arrogant, therefore, making me unlikeable. It was the beginning of a long road for me, but I was excited to play around with ideas and see what worked.

I was the newbie on the scene and there were many clique groups of comedians who didn't overly welcome new comics with warm open arms. Comics liked to test the newbies to see how long they would be sticking around. It wasn't until a good year in when you were seen to be taking it seriously and stand-up comedians became friends. When I joined the circuit, I noticed there were very few female comics, which unfortunately seemed to hinder rather than help me. I had suddenly entered a predominantly male world, and I hadn't been invited. Some of the more experienced comics didn't warm to my large presence and my very outspoken personality. But like all jobs, some people don't gel, while some become lifelong friends and everyone else in between.

Months were flying by, and I was very quickly learning new techniques and tricks to improve my craft whilst testing the waters, experiencing and experimenting with who I was. Being a naturally energetic person, didn't necessarily mean that was what I was meant to bring to the stage. It was all about knowing your audience, believing in what you were saying or doing and never taking yourself too seriously. I was receiving laughter and very positive feedback from audience members after seeing snippets of work I was beginning to create, so I knew I was on the right track. Writing good jokes was, in a way, the easy part; I always used real life experiences and could edit, engage and write surprising punchlines. Getting the audience to listen to my stories was easy too, I had an energy and a subject to grab their attention. It was being relatable and likeable that seemed to be my hurdle.

There was always a part of me that thought, fuck it. I should be able to wear what I want, talk about what I want, be who I want and do what I want. But like with many things in life, there was an unwritten rule that no one ever really talked about. And that was being relatable, unless you were playing an obvious OTT character, comedians and storytelling had to be relatable, so the audience to connect, I found, so challenging for such a long time because I was passionate about discussing true life events from my own experiences and how I felt about them, but audience members took one look at me and thought what I was talking about, whether it was never being able to find a boyfriend and heartbreak I felt, or stealing large quantities of smoked salmon, they thought it was all made up. This was a lesson every stand-up had to learn, being relatable as well as funny, and I was learning the hard way.

I was told that one day, in my everlasting learning experience, I would get that light bulb moment. This would be the moment when things would just fall into place and stand-up comedy, as long as you had the funny gene, would become a lot easier. I was aware that I was receiving a positive reaction from my gigs most of the time, which kept me going and made me look forward to finding out who I was as a performer, and wait for that light bulb moment.

But from the day I joined the London comedy scene, I had witnessed and experienced that some promoters, a few fellow comics, and audience members, treat some of the few female comics as idiots, pieces of meat and, quite literally, a joke. It was as though that was simply the way of the world and I had to accept it. I would feel myself anger, when certain promoters made a point in making sure the acts had the 'one female comedian' in one night. It was 2010 and I felt like I was suddenly back in the 1950s. Not all comedy nights worked that way, of course. But the ones that did must have been stuck in such a narrow-minded world where that one female act had to feel grateful to be put on their bill. When one female comedian to seven male comedians would play in the night, that one female would be introduced like it was a novelty act. Mentioning the word 'female' before introducing the name, was incredibly annoying. At a comedy club in Kentish Town, there was a transgender comedian trying out some new material, who I went on to do many gigs with in Brighton. I thought she was fantastic. Honest, raw and sharp with hilarious adlibs. The promoter came on stage to introduce me on after she had performed. The ignorant promoter announced, "Next we have a real woman," I never gigged for him again.

Ironically, the first ever heckle I received was from a woman. I had been on the circuit for around 4 months and I was warned that a first heckle is like your first kiss, you never quite forget it. Every comic reacts very differently depending on the heckle. Some choose to ignore. Some get aggressive. Some shoot them down with a genius one-liner. I found that some comedians addressed the heckler and used the story as material in their future sets. This was what I did with my first heckle. I was in a pub in South London where a very drunk elderly woman, with a crazy mop of curly orange hair, shouted from the back of the room; "They're only laughing 'cuz they wanna fuck you!"

I felt my entire body seize up as I went into shock and my mouth dried up. No one really prepares you for the feeling of your first heckle, and in that moment, it was a case of my mind going blank and every millisecond felt like a year. Then I suddenly thought of the perfect comeback: "Well, at least someone is getting fucked!" And with that, the small audience of twelve members burst into laughter. It felt good.

As time went by, I was noticing that I was only being heckled by women. I had a gig at the Comedy Store in Leicester Square where a group of six women booed me off stage. The very next day, I had a notification that a comment was left on one of my own personal YouTube clips of me performing. It was from one of the women who booed me saying they had come to see comedy and had to see me instead. I was taken aback that this person had spent the time to write this on my clip. I shed one tear, but then told myself that at least she remembered my name. Only a few months later, I was left more 'feedback' on the same YouTube clip. There, left under the name of 'SJP', which obviously made me think of the name Sarah Jessica Parker, so knew whoever it was, had cowardly hid who they were. The comment read: "I've had the displeasure of working with this girl, two months ago and she is nothing more than a deluded Bimbo." I felt scared not knowing who this person was and spent far too long wondering who could dislike me that much. I knew I had a good heart and I knew I was doing well in comedy, but this troll really got to me. I knew then I couldn't let comments on a computer screen get inside my already troubled mind.

I also received very interesting reactions when I told people I did stand-up comedy. I would often get the line: "But you don't look like a comedian." What was a comedian supposed to look like? I had been asking myself this question for months. Would I ever just fit in without being questioned or judged? It became more apparent that people seemed to be put into a box of what looks went with what career choice, and it really started to bug me. One venue held the comedy in a room upstairs and turning up early to prepare for my gig. The bartender didn't believe I was an act and thought I just wanted to get in to see the comedy for free so wouldn't let me up to prepare. It was infuriating. All I was there to do was to entertain and make people feel good. I wasn't there to think about my appearance or fit people's criteria of what a comedian should look like. There was a short period time I would regularly bump into a female comic who was up and coming and doing well with the crowd. She was a comic who wanted to portray herself as 'unattractive' and self-deprecating for the audience to sympathise. If that's the persona she wanted to portray then that was fair enough. But I started to notice comments of hatred she wrote on her Facebook page about women who were slim and attractive. 'Pretty girls have it easy in life' and 'Skinny girls get what they want'. I couldn't believe it. I wanted her to step inside my head for the day and make her realise that no matter what people looked like, it was people's mental health that was the real issue, but she was ignorant to that. I wasn't prepared to gain weight, change my appearance or apologise for how I looked. Being ridiculed for how I looked when I couldn't help it was one thing but having the anxiety and thoughts that entered my head daily was a completely different matter.

As time went by and the number of female comics grew on the scene, I felt like I was being taken more seriously as a performer in the world of stand-up. My stage time was getting longer; the audiences were getting bigger and I was starting to get paid gigs. Comedians got to know who I was on a more personal level, and my name and face was being remembered by regular audience members who followed the scene. I had a great gig opening for the 90s comedian Bob Mills who was just brilliant on stage, receiving an encore when he finished his 30-minute set after mine. And he was nice enough to offer me a lift home, and I'll always remember what he said to me when he dropped me off. "If you are unique, memorable, marketable, and professional, which you are, you have nothing to worry about."

Whilst I was still trying to figure out what kind of stand-up I was, and I waited waiting for that 'light bulb moment', I decided to focus and use some of the skills I had; creative writing. I remembered that first poem I wrote about my family and when I read it out at school. Throughout the years, I had written a lot of sombre poetry that helped me deal with sad times, but I made the decision to start writing comedy poetry which I could use in my sets. At the time, there was literally only ONE comic performing poetry on the circuit, and not only did I think he was brilliant, but I was also surprised there weren't more people around with this idea.

The Bitterness of Singleton City

Being single was shit, in every miniscule way,
I even missed the bad stuff in boyfriends, like him farting and pushing my head under the duvet.

Weekends are the worst. Sunday morning together having a snooze,
No longer feeling his hard-on from behind, no longer feeling his premature ooze.

So I gorged on greasy pizzas, thinking, "Fuck it, I may as well eat the lot."
I'd be crying out of self-pity, so I'd reach for some dirty panties to wipe away the snot.

When I am horny, I'd reach for the draw, the rabbit kept things flowing,
Duracell batteries were expensive, but luckily, they kept on going and going and going.

Single life was shit, ticking that marital status box was a dread,

*because I feel like a spinster. I think I'd rather have ticked
that widowed box instead.*

Dating was a nightmare, they had turned into interviews,
*Quick fire questions of 'do you fit the criteria?' Come on,
just break the bad news.*

*My last date was gay. Christ, what a night. He was just
trying to prove himself straight.*
*He asked me if I had any gay experiences. I asked him, and
he said, "Yes, I've had eight!"*

*Being single is shit. Friday nights, my sheets were no
longer wet,*
*I'd started scrolling my phone for names, scraping the
barrel of what I could get.*

*But I didn't fancy any of them, so all I expected was a
Facebook poke.*
*Maybe one day I'd feel the weight of a handsome funny
young bloke.*

*So, for now, it is just me, the rabbit and Denzel (my 10-inch
black laptop), having a flooze.*
I am sure one day I'd wake up to some premature ooze.

Back on January 18, 2010, only a few short weeks into the
world of stand-up comedy, I was having dinner with my new
friend Samar, catching up on the first few gigs we had
experienced since leaving the Comedy School in November. I
was also filling her in since we last saw each other about a new
job I had been offered, working as a private PA for a hotel
owner. I was given a private room in the Hotel in Blackfriars,
where my job was to pay old bills, sort out road congestion
charges and was even asked to import the owner's dogs from
Dubai to London. I didn't have a clue what I was doing, but
strangely, having to do it on my own made me manage myself
better. Dealing with the owner, however, was a different story.
A 55-year-old unmarried man that reminded me of Danny
DeVito's character, The Penguin, was quite possibly the rudest

man I had ever met in my life. Having to sit and eat dinner with him in the hotel with Rosie the manager, who I got on really well with, would look at me in a way like she was apologising for me having to be there next to him. He would fling his food around, shouted at the staff and demanded whatever he wanted with chewed up food all around his slobbering mouth. The only silver lining I had while I was working there was that my office was next door to a help desk that sat a guy called Stephan. He was from Germany, physically wasn't really my type, but I found him funny and interesting. His accent was stronger than any other German I had met and as he told me stories about his travels moving from place to place, I suddenly saw a relationship that could be brief, but fun.

When telling Samar, the gossip over dinner that night, she said, "I bet you will be dating him by Valentine's Day." Just as we were finishing off our meals, my phone beeped. It was David. Samar knew everything about my relationship with David and the heart ache I was still dealing with. When the text came through and she saw my face lit up, she took my hands and just smiled.

Over the next few weeks, working with Stephan every day, of course, we inevitably got closer. I was always honest from the start that I didn't want a relationship and I assumed he didn't want one either due to his travel plans. As the dates grew, I couldn't help but compare him to David. I still loved him so much, and my heart was well and truly David's, and I was closed to anyone else. Having David pop up on my phone from time to time always gave me some hope that he obviously was still thinking of me and could still love me. I knew, of course, he was still with Laura, and I still had that gut feeling that they wouldn't last much longer.

I was gigging on a regular basis around London, and my poetry started to be used a lot more frequently within my sets. I couldn't help but write a poem about my experience with the German Stephan, Luckily, he found the poem very funny, and was even flattered I used it in a set I did for Valentine's Day. Samar was right, we were together having fun just as she predicted, but I made sure Stephan knew it would never be more than some short-term fun and companionship.

When I Slept With a German

I was fed up with English boyfriends,
So I ventured elsewhere.

As long as he wasn't Welsh,
I really didn't care.

So I went to a club and asked every guy to speak,
I wanted an accent, maybe Russian, French or Greek!

Then from the crowd, I saw a sensible looking blonde.
This chap was a German, so of course I was fond.

He was tall, confident, chiselled and strong.
But through my beer goggles, I could sense this was all wrong.

Remember the dad from the Munster's, the man's name was Herman.
They must have been related, 'cuz he looked like the German.

This guy was serious yet fun and loved the thrill of the chase.
But unfortunately, didn't understand humour if it hit him in the face.

German accents are funny old things, with this T H turned into Ts.
And the poor bugger, his Ws were always pronounced as Ds.

The passion in the bedroom was always turned up a notch.
But he always tried to shove his cock up my ass instead of my crotch!

When he came, he'd shout "DIE SCHEISEE HAT DUN!"
I don't know what this means, but I knew he was unloading his gun.

We had an intense relationship that fizzled after half a year.
His passion overtook mine that much was just clear.

My bum was sore, and I needed time on my own to rest.
We are just good friends now, I think that's for the best.

Stephan never mentioned my last line about just being good friends, but I had always told him I couldn't fully commit emotionally, and I was given the impression he was on the same page with his travel plans. After my set on Valentine's Day, we went for a drink and he had bought me a single blue rose. He said it took him ages to find and the same for finding me too. Stephan was feeling more for me than I had anticipated, and I remember feeling concerned, as I didn't want to hurt him.

It was March, and we were both still working at the hotel. I was staying at Stephan's from time to time. One night after work, I was on Oxford Street waiting for the bus to go to Stephan's house, when I saw David on bus looking right at me, head still turning toward me as it drove past. I was on the phone talking to Stephan, when I accidently blurted out what I had just seen.

"I've got to go," I said, as I abruptly hung up while I heard him starting to shout down the phone.

"Don't you dar…"

I didn't care. The bus stopped at a red light, so I started running towards it. I was never a strong runner, but I had to sprint to make it on time. The long bendy bus had pulled into the next stop, the front and back doors opened, and I jumped on and found myself spontaneously standing at the back of the bus, to see David's face just sitting there, looking shocked to see what I had just done. All I could manage to say was, "I don't know what I'm doing here." I really didn't. All I knew is how much I loved him.

Three nights later, after apologising to Stephan and explaining again where I stood in the relationship, we went to a club in the West End to have some fun together. Outside, when we were leaving the venue, a man felt me up from behind and I confronted him. He punched me so hard in the face, I was knocked out and fell to the ground like a domino piece.

Everything was caught on camera and it showed the man running from the scene. Once he had hit me and I lay in the streets unconscious, the police and ambulance were called. All I remember was waking up in hospital and asking for David. When I regained all consciousness, I cried as I felt a large egg sized lump on the back of my skull. I was released from hospital the next day and was told to sleep. But I couldn't. The pain in my head was unbearable and all I wanted to do was call David.

Two weeks later, now money was a little more stable, still thinking about David, I made the decision to get a tattoo. David and I both planned to get 'TAURUS' written in Arabic when we first met. When the day finally came, it was David that went ahead, and got it done on his back and I had chickened out. So, the day came in 2010, once my swollen head was almost back to normal, I walked into a tattoo parlour just off Tottenham Court Road, where I went and got the tattoo I was meant to get on my right wrist in 2008. When Stephan saw what I had done, he knew exactly why I did it and he went ballistic. He told me I was stupid for holding onto the past, and I needed to let go and move on.

Still seeing Stephan a week before my birthday and trying my best not to think about David, he invited me along to the May festival in Germany to meet his parents. I knew I shouldn't have gone, but David was still with Laura, and I had been dating the Stephan for almost four months and was really trying to move on. The May festival was held over the end of April in Cologne, where people celebrated through the night to see in the month of May. Once we were in Cologne, we were ploughed with shots of Jägermeister and got horribly drunk. After the midnight hour and May had arrived, we walked back to his parents' house having a tremendous row in the middle of a field. To this day, I can't even remember what it was about, but I knew I had to end it. Stephan walked off and I was left alone in a beautiful, lush green field, where I found myself completely alone. I looked up at the sky and I remember seeing millions of sparkling stars shimmering over the pitch-black endless space. As I looked up, I did something out of the ordinary, I said a prayer. I prayed that I would hear from David. I prayed I would receive a sign that he still loved me. I hadn't heard from him in so long, and the pain I felt missing him consumed me once again. I finally caught up with Stephan and what felt like forever traipsing through fields, we got back to his parents' house it was gone 3 am. As I checked the time on my phone, there it was—a text from David and all it said was 'hello'. He had sent it an hour earlier.

May 5, my birthday. Another year older and still as foolish as ever. A group of us, including Stephan, went out in Hoxton for a night out. Samar was there, shaking her head and rolling her eyes at why I was still dating Stephan. While a group of us were out dancing, my phone buzzed, and it was David. He was wishing me a happy birthday and through my hazy vodka filled mind, I decided to invite him along, not even thinking about the consequences. But David didn't show. It was nothing more than another passing text.

A few days later, David texted me again asking to meet him as he had bought me a birthday gift. I felt a whole array of emotions. Anger, that he was with Laura and buying me presents but a little smug that he wanted to see me. Upset, that we weren't together and confused as to why he was even buying me birthday presents in the first place. But mostly, I was happy to hear from the only person I loved so much. So, I went to meet him at Ryan's bar on Church Street Stoke Newington, where we had lived together before. I purposely turned up fifteen minutes late, feeling butterflies like I always felt when I knew I was going to see David. I got there to see him with a drink waiting for me and a gift bag. Nothing felt awkward, nothing was wrong between us, and it felt like we had never broken up. David bought me two presents. One made me smile because he knew how much I wanted my own cat. It was a paper bag, with a toy cat's tail that hung outside and inside the mechanical cat wiggled around the bag, making it appear it was a real cat trying to escape. The other was a coffee coaster with the words, 'To the sexiest woman on the planet'. I felt frustration that if he thought that about me, why weren't we back together. But I accepted the gifts and we had a catch up over some drinks. There was still that undeniable spark between us and the chemistry that no one could top.

I wasn't needed to work at the hotel anymore, so my relationship with Stephan very quickly fizzled out once I had left. Looking back, I had hurt him and I shouldn't have dated him for as long as I did. Once I was out of work again, David and I were seeing each other a little more often. A coffee here, a cinema trip there, all the while there was still that unspoken elephant in the room that he was still with her. After almost ten weeks of us seeing each other for drinks after work and constant messages, I was sick of sharing David. I never once felt like 'the other woman', even though to some, I would have been. But I had given my heart to David the day I met him, and while I knew deep down he still loved me. I knew he was going back home to Laura for a reason, he wasn't ready to be with me, knowing how unpredictable and unstable my emotions and moods were for so long.

Out of the blue, one day when I checked up on Laura's still public Facebook page, it showed photos of her moving out of the flat she had been living in with David for all those months. I felt a sudden rush of adrenalin, wondering if David had told her what we had been doing and she had finished with him. But there was no sign of anger or upset on her page. Just excitement to be getting her own place, further out of London where property was cheaper.

It got to the point where I finally told David that we clearly still had feelings for one another, and I asked him to end it with Laura. He wouldn't, and my heart was breaking all over again. I made a risky decision to contact Laura and tell her about my meet ups with David. Not to hurt, but because I couldn't handle the situation and the pain anymore. Surprisingly, she gave me her number, and asked me to text her all of the dates David and I had spent together. Of course, I knew she wouldn't believe me, but it was the only proof I had. Within hours, I received the inevitable call from David. As he shouted down the phone from the mess I had made and told me he never wished to see me again. I begged to make him understand that I couldn't share him anymore, and that his relationship with Laura was a joke right from the very start. But he didn't want to know. I texted him over the next few days, with no replies and no response, I felt like I was back to square one. He didn't want anything to do with me. I had lost him once before and now I had lost him again. There were times when I felt pangs of pure rage. Rage that David hadn't sorted things out himself, and that I was made to look like someone who had broken up a relationship. I may have been responsible for the initial break up, but it was David who was living a lie, when for months I begged him to tell her about all the time we were spending together. I knew he loved me, but he just couldn't be with me.

To make matters worse, I received an extremely vicious email from Laura a few days later. It was a hot summer's morning and I had started a temp reception job in Mayfair. Assuming Laura got my email address from my comedy website, she sent me a long harsh message that came as quite a shock. Words within the email shouted out at me. She didn't express how angry or upset she was at me or David, but instead just filled the page with abusive and offensive remarks about me as a person. As the words sprung at me like hot darts out of the screen, I felt surprisingly calm to begin with. I knew she was just unleashing her upset and I was right person to let it out on. However, as her words got stronger and more personal, a cold cocktail of anger and revenge started lingering inside me. Emotions were whizzing though my veins as all I felt was this other woman who knew nothing about me was doing her very best to make me feel so worthless. To me, she was the other women who had spent the last sixteen months with the only man I loved. To her, I was probably the other woman, but all three of us in that messy situation knew that for some reason, David and I couldn't let each other go. Without a hesitation, I decided right there and then to print out the email, and bleed all over with red ink. I circled every incorrect opinion that she had written, every incorrect fact and every obscene judgement. The page was covered in thick red circles. I never wrote any personal comment or remark about her, I never mentioned David, I just wanted the facts clear. The truth was out in the open, free to do as she pleased. I then scanned it and emailed it back to her. I knew she would have read it, and I knew then and there that I would never hear from her again.

While I was temping in Mayfair, I was surrounded by rather peculiar people. The manager would often walk through the reception area completely naked from the staff showers to his office. He would walk past, holding the towel to dry his hair whilst everything else hung out for me to see. It was a family run business so there was no HR I could go to. So instead, I just took it for what it was; odd. His PA wasn't particularly nice either. She was continually getting plastic surgery done here, there, and everywhere and often had entire parts of her face and body bandaged up like an Egyptian mummy. She would sometimes stand right over me and ask me what the hell I was doing there in the office as I didn't belong there as I had my other 'career'. After exactly six weeks working for the company, I was fired, or should I say, 'asked to leave' because I 'didn't fit in'. I discovered that the PA had told our boss if he didn't get rid of me, she would leave herself. With no HR to turn to, I grabbed my bag and walked out. The very week I left, a girl I had worked with at another job I had been fired from, messaged me, and asked if I fancied going along with her and her friends on a last-minute girl's holiday to Ibiza. This was one of those perfect moments when I just thought, *Fuck it*. It was just what I needed.

At the airport, I met the two other girls who were invited to come along to Ibiza, Carley and Jenny, who worked with my friend. We all got some drinks and got to know each other. With what I discovered within the next hour, almost knocked me off my chair. I knew that Carley and Jenny also worked with my friend for *The Sun* Newspaper, and they had been updated on my painful David story. The girls' offices were all being refurbished, and here was a seating area near the girls for the project managers and designers to stay. It turned out, one of the guys working on the project there, who they sometimes spoke to, was David himself. My David. It hadn't clicked to my friend as she didn't know that the David I had been talking about looked like, so it wasn't until she had told the David at her work about our Ibiza plans, and mentioning me and the comedy I did where it all fell into place, and he asked, "You don't mean Naomi Hefter, do you?" I couldn't believe what a small world it was.

The night we turned up in Ibiza, we decided to just have some drinks in a late-night bar, rather than do a big club. Within half an hour of going into a little bar with extremely strong drinks and free shots to get us on our way, we got chatting to four American guys. One of them, Alex, who even though lived in New York, was half Russian, half Hungarian. Having Hungarian roots myself, we had something in common, and he was exactly my type with blue eyes thick blonde hair and a friendly face which gave him similarities to Leonardo DiCaprio.

Four hours in, and the group of us were drinking and dancing and taking lots of photos together. Only one of the four Americans had a girlfriend and he was a real gentleman, not trying it on with anyone or being disrespectful to his girlfriend back in the States. All four were genuinely good guys. The four night and five days in Ibiza were just amazing. Dancing, drinking, laughing and sunbathing with the weight of the world off my shoulders. I was transported to another planet and I loved every minute of it. I had never experienced a holiday romance, but with Alex, I quickly discovered how intense the whole thing was. Lust grew rapidly fast and being in Ibiza together melted away any problem or worry we had in the real world. It was a perfect bubble of undeniable bliss that would inevitably have to end.

After five days of partying with the girls, with the added cherry of my holiday romance with Alex, saying goodbye to him and Ibiza was hard. I knew it had to end but he certainly took me away from thinking about David. He was the perfect distraction. We didn't want it to end but of course, once we were both back in the real world, it fizzled out and feelings faded. But for a short time in my far away world from David made me question if I could ever meet someone that could get me over him once and for all.

Diary Extract – October 2, 2010

On my way to another boring temp job, I was lucky enough to meet a cat called Bob and his owner, James, on the 73 bus. I had seen them around a few times, but on this occasion, when they jumped on the bus, I asked James if I could stroke Bob. James was very protective of him, unsurprisingly. They suddenly became very well known when they were offered a book deal about their unique story. They already had a following around Covent Garden and Angel, where James sold The Big Issue, so I was excited when they jumped on the bus that day. It's funny how life can change. From being reliant on drugs and being homeless, to now living a good life together and doing well. From meeting a stray cat where such a strong bond was born, I felt really happy that they found each other. Wherever they are living now, I hope James and Bob are doing well. I heard a movie is being made about them too. I look forward to seeing it.

Christmas was always a painful time for me. As a child, I longed for a traditional Christmas sat around a large table with a golden crispy turkey, and all the bowls of different vegetables and potatoes where you could help yourself. But I never had a Christmas like that. As the years went by, the festive period got worse and worse when Bill came into the picture. I had to take emotional and mental abuse from him, and finally, when my mother let him throw me out on to the streets, I was free from his torture. But the Christmas of 1999, at the age of 16, I was completely alone. A friend I was at college with, kindly invited me to spend Christmas with her and her family that year. I will never forget sitting around the table and experiencing my first traditional family Christmas. All sat around a table with all the food, trimmings, traditions and laughter, I felt a sense of sadness inside but so grateful to be there amongst such happy, good-natured people. Ironically, they bought me The Grinch on video. I loved Jim Carrey, so I loved the gift, I found the movie hilarious. My friend and her family really made me feel welcome that year, it was one of those moments I wondered if I could recreate that very feeling for myself one day.

It wasn't until three years later, 2002 where my mother and I had just got back in contact, and I was anticipating the first Christmas back with her after so much time without talking. It was 2002 and I had just finished my first semester at university. Everything was still raw between us and resentment still clung on to me. From the day I was thrown out, neither of us had ever really sat down and discussed anything about it. For three years, I kept asking myself how a mother could let her abusive husband throw their daughter out onto the streets. So, there I was, back in Cheltenham on Christmas day and Bill was no longer there. My mother had recently separated from him, and I thought Christmas without him could possibly be like old times when I was a child and it was just me and my mother in happier times that we had for a short time together. My mother and Bill had two children, the first when I was thirteen and the second when I was fourteen. I never really got to form a strong relationship with them as I hadn't seen them properly for years and they were still so young. As all four of us spent Christmas day together, it felt forced and a little awkward as nothing had been talked about since I was thrown out,

On Boxing Day, with a day of watching TV and eating too much, a chewed-up wet sticky jellybean was found under the cushion of the sofa by my mother. Holding it right to my face, she hissed, "You little dirty slut." I was automatically blamed before her two infant children.

"How could you think I would spit out a chewed-up jelly bean and put it on your sofa? I'm 19, not 5!" I cried out feeling my blood starting to boil. How she could even think to accuse me and blame me when it was obviously my brother or sister who were young enough to innocently do something like that. As it turned out, it was my little brother who had done it. He told his mummy he hadn't liked the flavour and spat it out. Through my defensive tears and clenched jaw, I glared at my mother who appeared to just look right through me rather than apologise. Tears ran down my face and I missed my new life at university. I had made some great new friends and most of all, I had left Cheltenham. To my mother, I was physically free from her and the past, but emotionally and mentally, I hadn't left, and I couldn't let go and move on. Cheltenham, my mother, my father and Bill were sticking onto me one way or another. I left my mother's house the day after Boxing Day and went back to Worcester, it was a ghost town around campus, but I didn't care. My friends would be back in less than a week, and I had all the spare time and space to write some poems, play some music and not have my mother around to beat me down with her accusations and vile names.

Exactly one year later, the Christmas of 2003, my mother and I were still in contact, but barely. Now Bill was fully out of the picture, she was going through a partying phase with a new friend of hers. Most new singles have a new haircut or lose some weight, but not my mother. She had started talking recreational drugs, and going to clubs around Bristol and Birmingham, returning early mornings the following day. Her new friend, who was heavily into the party scene, dated men much younger than her 50 years and just seemed like a pretty bad influence on my mother. I was worried, but my mother insisted she was just having fun. On Christmas day, 2003, my brother and sister were with Bill, and my mother and I planned to have a day of movies, a steak each for dinner and a bottle of champagne to share. I was in the bath when her party friend came around. As I rinsed my hair, I heard the pop of a cork and a 'cheers' from the living room as they opened and drank the saved champagne for themselves. Within an hour, they were both pissed and went out for the day. I was left alone that Christmas and utterly disappointed my mother could do that to me when we should have been building a relationship.

So, six years later in 2010, when me and my mother had somehow built up a relationship, and she knew how heartbroken I was over David, there was effort made on her part. She met me at the train station, made me a nice dinner on Christmas Eve and we watched movies to see Christmas day in at midnight. But unfortunately, she had to work on Christmas day itself, and my brother and sister where with Bill, so I spent the day alone. I never resented her for having to work, I understood, but that day, sat alone, for me was the worst. I put Beyoncé in concert on the TV that aired for a Christmas day special. Thousands of people across the country were ready to tune into that one-off treat of showing her concert on the TV. As I sat in the living room, listening to the beautiful song of *Halo* sung so well by Beyoncé, tears streamed down my face. I wept as I felt pain ripping through my heart as I missed David so much. We weren't even talking, let alone any closer to being together. All I wanted was him there with me. And I didn't even know if or when I would hear from him again.

2011

"The Name's Jenkins, Naomi Jenkins."

New Year's Day, 2011, I went through my Facebook friends list, and deleted negative and unwanted people from it. I wanted a mental spring clean of my life to try and start the year with positivity. It wasn't until the spring of 2011, when I was told about the then famous logo: KEEP CALM AND CARRY ON that originated from the war. Shirts, mugs, stickers and coasters were suddenly the thing to buy, especially in the tourist shops of London. It had been six months after I had sprung cleaned my Facebook contacts that I was informed about a link that I needed to check out. There was an entire page dedicated to all kinds of items people could buy with the logo: KEEP CALM BUT NAOMI HEFTER DEFRIENDED ME. As I gazed opened eyed to the merchandise, I didn't know either to be frightened, amused, shocked or simply flattered. Of course, I had to order some for myself! How could I not!? I bought a t-shirt and a sheet of 100 stickers. I knew this was a story I could potentially use in my comedy set but I was just so curious who would set up the page. I sat and tried to remember all the people I had deleted in January, but I just couldn't think who would do this bizarre random thing. When I used the story during my later gigs, audience members would ask me if I ever found out who the person was. I never did.

I once heard that meeting a true friend in London was hard. I had already experienced the feeling of 'this person will be in my life for a very long time', with David. So, to experience the same feeling when I met my friend for life, Catherin Povinelli, I felt very lucky indeed. We met at the yearly event of the Funny Women competition, in Leicester Square Theatre. This was a company that focused on showcasing new up and coming female comedians on the circuit across Britain. As a group of us prepared in the green room ready to perform, I noticed Catherine stand out amongst the other girls. She was dressed quite bizarrely, wearing a mishmash of multi colours; Purple tights under bright blue denim shorts and a red American style football shirt slung on the top half of her body. I was doing my makeup in the mirror and through the reflection I remember thinking that she was quite outrageous as I watched her, suddenly began to hump the floor. All the girls were getting ready and keeping to themselves, so I decided to talk to this new interesting person. We were the same age, exactly four months apart to the day and she was originally from New York. She had been living in London for the last year and had started stand up about 9 months after me. We had only been talking for a short time, but we got on straight away and I looked forward to seeing her perform. She introduced herself as 'Povs' on stage, short for her surname Povinelli, so I made the decision to call her that from then on.

Once Povs had been on stage, I knew she was the right person to ask if she wanted to do a double hander for the Edinburgh Festival with me the following year in 2012. This would involve us performing thirty minutes each in an hour slot given to us. I had roughly thirty minutes of material and I felt ready to put on a show. It may have only been half the time on stage, but it would also half the cost of everything we would need to pay for. We met over coffee a few days after the Funny Women competition, and we had talked about how we viewed comedy and what we wanted from it all. We were very much on the same wavelength, plus we just clicked as we were quite similar people. I really liked this girl. We had chemistry, a connection, so we decided to have a night out and go on a 'first date', as we put it.

Going out with a new friend for the first time felt like going on a first date. Povs turned up at my place and we had some drinks. With no plan in mind, we soon discovered that we both had a passion for old school dance music, especially Trance from the 90s. So, we very randomly went to a club called Hidden, in Vauxhall, which neither of us had been to before to. Growing up, I had always enjoyed trance music. I knew that trance was seen in a certain way with its drug scene, but I just simply loved the music and didn't feel the need to take drugs, with its unique sound Trance gave me its own euphoric feeling. When I heard DJs like Paul Oakenfold, Signum and Faithless, the classic tunes from the 90s gave me so much energy, I was often asked what drug I had been taking.

As we approached the club, we looked at each other as we heard the hard, fast beat of trance seeping through the building walls. Once we got to the entrance, I spontaneously decided to do something to try and save us money. I confidently walked up to the female bouncer and gushed, "Hi, we are on the guest list, the name's Naomi Hefter!" As the bouncer looked down at her list, she finally got to a name.

"Naomi Jenkins?" she said, looking up at me, if I was indeed Naomi Jenkins.

"Yes, I'm Naomi Jenkins, that's me," I quickly replied, without stumbling my words. I couldn't believe that this was even happening, and that it had worked even with me saying my correct name to begin with. But as the female bouncer heard me say Naomi Jenkins, we walked right in and once firmly inside, Povs and I exploded with laughter.

Seeing the lasers and the ravers wearing their furry boots really did transport me back to the 90s. Povs and I were on our merry way, having a dance and getting to know each other. I was really enjoying myself with the new person in my life.

Before we knew it, Povs had become a firm friend of mine. The weeks had merged into one big night out. I honestly couldn't differentiate all the nights out we had together. Going to all the major clubs, trying out new and fun places to experience. We had made up funny dance routines, like retro gym moves and performed them in the middle of the dance floors, which always got a crowd around us and even joining in. We created so many hilarious memories, making up characters and silly names for ourselves, and the people we met on nights out. Each night, a photo album would be created on Facebook so we could distinguish each night before they all merged into one.

When we weren't out partying, we had cinema nights, where we would purposely turn up early to dance around the empty cinema. When we stayed in, Povs would come over to mine and watch episodes of the fashion comedy sitcom of the 90s, *Absolutely Fabulous,* and I would cook her the only decent dish I could make, Hungarian chicken paprika or we would order Chinese dumplings from the local restaurant, and chat for hours about family and love and where we wanted to go in life.

We had been to almost every major nightclub in and around London, when Povs and I suddenly realised, we had never been to Pasha in Victoria. When we bought tickets online to go one Friday night, we turned up to find a two-hour long queue that consisted of girls and guys that looked no older than 17, each one holding a bottle of Smirnoff Ice. We had wanted to go to Pasha for so long, but we knew then this was not the night for us. We headed back to our first date club, Hidden, and came up with a cunning plan along the way. It was one of those nights where we may have been low on cash, but we always managed to have such a fun time one way or another. We headed to the entrance at Hidden, clutching our Pasha Tickets, pretending we were about to head into Pasha itself. Once we got to the ticket office, the guys said that we were at the wrong venue. "This isn't Pasha?" I asked, in a badly muddled accent of German and English I often put on to sound as though I didn't know where on earth I was. And surprisingly, the plan worked even though I was useless at accents. The doormen took our confusion and puzzled faces, thinking we had spent our money on tickets that we wanted for Hidden and let us walk in with our Pasha tickets. We were laughing hard as we got in with the incorrect tickets. We had a blast dancing the night away and we were even recognised by two guys who had seen us at a comedy gig we had done a few weeks earlier. When 5am hit, and it was time to leave, we waited at Waterloo station for the tubes to open. At this point, we had met two very random people, one of which named me Helen of Troy and the other claimed to be out with his grandmother as he pointed at an old lady drinking tea alone waiting for a train. After squeezing myself through the shut metal bars into the locked-up toilets in Waterloo and stealing some plastic flowers that were chained to the sink, I gave them to my new fan who got down on one knee and proposed, still calling me Helen of Troy. With that, I was engaged to a stranger, eating a Big Mac with a grandma and enjoyed watching Povs run around the station like the Tasmanian Devil.

As 2011 went by, Povs and I started to plan our double hander for our show at Edinburgh Festival 2012, and all the while, our friendship became stronger and stronger. Before we knew it, we were never seen without the other on the comedy scene. We had each other's backs and supporting each other's gigs. We purposely planned gigs to do together at the same venue to support each other or just go and watch each other try out new material in preparation for our Edinburgh show. We were a proper little double act and I felt completely at one with her. We were two peas in a pod and any time we weren't together at the same comedy club, comics would ask where the other one was. We were simply two single girls with our own issues, having a blast. I had finally felt some of that loneliness disperse from my life.

The first six months of 2011, before meeting Povs, I could only picture a hand full of moments, like photographs. Days and weeks around those mental photographs, were just a sea of diluted grey haze that linked the days together, before something significant happened that year, like meeting Povs.

My first memory or 'photograph' was from the first Sunday night in January 2011. I was in bed when the doorbell rang. Lo and behold, it was David. Over the intercom, he asked me to come down to see him; he didn't want to come up for some reason. So, feeling the butterflies flutter all over again, I made my way downstairs, makeup free and feeling the cold winter air through the long sheer fabric of my 70s style nighty that floated around me. I opened the door and he was standing there, crying. Two tears fell from his eyes as he just said the words 'I'm sorry'. I asked if he wanted to come in, but he still said no. He noticed I had cut my hair and then he left. That was it. He was gone again.

The second memory I have, was later on in January and I was sitting with my doctor. The time had come, and I felt ready to speak to the doctor to understand why I struggled to face so many days, and why I felt such sadness and felt so anxious about my future. She spoke to me about how long I had been feeling the way I had, and asked me to fill out a form there and then.

I remember having to choose between 'highly agree and highly disagree' to questions like 'Do you avoid socialising with people?' and 'Do you feel there is no way forward in life?'. I cried a lot, I wanted to spill out everything I had been feeling for so many years. The pain, the fear, the anger, the shoplifting I had been doing, the feeling of giving up, the panic I felt when I thought about my future. Instead, I just quietly ticked away at the form, feeling like I had the weight of the world on my shoulders. She told me she suspected I was suffering from depression and anxiety but advised me to refer myself to see someone who dealt with mental health issues, just like when I was 22. I was also prescribed a course of tablets called Citalopram. I didn't like the idea of having to take tablets to 'function' in my day-to-day life, but the doctor advised to take a 20mg pill a day for six months to see how I felt. I was to return to her in three months and redo the form I had just filled out. That moment in my life was so informal, so detached, so quick, yet it was a moment that changed my life forever.

Days and weeks around those two memories had vanished. Looking back, it was a possibility I had starting to focus on getting better, so unimportant things never stayed in my mind. Days just slipped on by and before I knew it, it was March and I had started working for some tax advisors in the West End, doing some admin and reception work. I had been taking Citalopram for eight weeks, and it had made me extremely hyperactive and highly energetic. I had gone from not getting out of bed to feeling I could conquer the world. However, the job I had started was a permanent role, and I had already received two verbal warnings for being so hyperactive and outrageous. Looking back, I should have spoken to someone there about the medication I was on, but I didn't want to tell a soul. I felt embarrassed and ashamed, and didn't think for a moment that anyone would understand why I was taking daily medication.

April, May, June, the months drifted on by and I had slipped into a routine of working, gigging, entering competitions, writing new material and thinking about heading to Edinburgh Festival for the first time that summer, to perform what they call 'open spots'. I had been performing 5-minute gigs in London, so I thought there was no harm in giving it a go and testing the water up in Scotland. It also gave me something to look forward to and focus on. Men weren't a part of my life; it was a time where it was just me, work and comedy.

The beginning of summer had approached, and I was heading to Romford in Essex for the first time to take part in a comedy competition called *Jokers*. I did a pretty good gig, throwing in a new joke about people walking too slowly in the streets, which went down well. After I had been on stage, I pulled my set apart and criticised myself as I always did. I decided to stay until the end, considering I didn't really have anything to go home to. I didn't realise there was a headline act coming on to close the night, a beatboxer no less. What appeared to be a shy guy I had noticed earlier that night, turned out to be an incredibly talented performer as he closed the gig with a very memorable and very impressive beatboxing set. His stage name was Philippic, cleverly due to the fact his name was Phil and the word meant 'attack of the mouth'. He sat down and chatted to the promoter, and I just felt I had to approach him to congratulate him on his set. As I guessed, he was a shy, modest guy when I complimented him on his beatboxing, which only made him more attractive to me. I remember noticing he had the most wonderful shade of green in his eyes and I was quite mesmerised by him. I gave him my number, and as I was on my way home on the train, he had already messaged me telling me he was happy to have met me. Keen, but not desperate or sleazy. Perfect.

Fast forward eight weeks and we were a couple, and things were running quite smoothly. He worked in a small bar in Essex, which was more like a family community centre, so I went along quite often, just got to know the locals and chatted away to everyone while Phil finished his shift. I was also introduced to his parents and they were the nicest parents I had met. Open and not afraid to show affection towards each other and towards Phil.

It was the beginning of a great summer, and one morning after Phil had stayed at my place, we were on the 73-bus heading towards the West End when I saw him—it was David at a bus stop on the opposite side of the road. He was just sitting there alone waiting. My heart stopped. I wanted to just jump off the bus and run to him. But before I knew it, he was out of sight as I was driven away.

On Friday 29th July, three days before I was to head to Edinburgh Festival for the first time to do some open spots. I had just performed a gig near Finsbury Park, where there were literally only two audience members to perform to, which left me feeling incredibly deflated. I always felt foolish after a quiet or bad gig and went straight home to feel sorry for myself, but that day was different. I got chatting to two men who were out together drinking at the upstairs bar. They invited me to join them, and my instincts told me to stay and have a drink. After an hour or so, with some laughter and banter that cheered me up, they mentioned they were going to a restaurant where they knew the owner. That owner happened to be Atik, the owner of Yum Yums on Church Street. David and I knew Atik pretty well as we lived opposite the restaurant during our year living together in 2008. We would often go in and have 2-4-1 cocktails on a Thursday after work and ate there on special occasions. So, with the convenience of a taxi ride home and more amusement from the guys, I joined them. Plus, it would have been nice to have a catch up with Atik. Since seeing him, he had won the best Thai restaurant in Britain on Gordon Ramsay's *The F Word.*

When we all turned up, we had some cocktails and I was happy to get the disappointing gig out of my mind. An hour later, the restaurant was about to close so the guys suggested drinks in the pub next door. We literally stepped out of the door of Yum Yums when I almost fell into a passer-by. It was David. I was stunned. He was with a tall bald guy and a short blonde girl. I instantly assumed David was dating the girl and as the two strangers walked further on, my knotted-up stomach and bitter voice sneered, and asked David if that was his girlfriend. David didn't reply and walked away to catch up with the two-mystery people. I stood around the restaurant and waited for Atik to lock up when I saw David, alone, walking back toward me. He stopped and stood in front of me and said nothing. All I could manage was, "What are you doing on my turf?"

He asked me to join his two friends who had headed to the Lion pub, right in the middle of Church Street. I said my good byes to the guys I had met and thanked them for making, what was a crappy night, really fun.

As I went to the loo in the Lion, the unknown blonde girl David was with followed me into the toilets and told me that she didn't know David well, but she could tell he still loved me. The night had been a whirlwind of catching up, music and dancing together. It was just like the old times. As the night went on, David and I were dancing away in a late-night bar to Ray Charles, and it was like we had never broken up. It was one of those amazingly unplanned surprises that happen once in a while. The next morning, I woke up bleary eyed, fully clothed in my bed with David holding my hand. We hadn't kissed, we didn't speak, we just lay there. I was home. This colossal, monumental feeling took over my heart and it all felt just right again. I knew there and then I would have to end it with Phil. I wasn't prepared to lead anyone else on again.

I headed up to Edinburgh three days later. I had booked a flight there through EasyJet as it was cheaper and obviously a lot faster than the train. I had never in my life flown alone before, and I suddenly found myself feeling very grown up. Checking in through security, making sure I was in the correct terminal, I sat and waited to board. Walking out and up the metal stairs to board the plane, I felt eyes upon me. I saw the pilot and his co-pilot, pointing at me through the dark windows of the plane. As the plane took off, I re read the same line of my magazine over and over as felt the butterflies in my stomach. Taking off always made me nervous but once we were up in the air, an airhostess approached me and asked me to walk with her to the front of the plane. I remember feeling strangely calm about that request and didn't question why she needed me. Before I knew it, I was sitting in the cockpit of the plane being introduced to the pilot. He had requested I join him, as he had seen me board and wanted to ask me out. I was flattered, but for a 5'9" girl being crumpled into the cockpit; the pilot was packed inside neatly like a folded sardine and couldn't have been any taller than Kylie Minogue. And how could I possibly date a pilot when I had bumped into David only days before.

When I arrived in Edinburgh, David had left me several text messages. I guessed that after the night we had and how obvious it was that I still loved him, I was now suddenly out of his reach.

Turning up to the Edinburgh Fringe, one of the largest arts festivals in the world, for the first time, was overwhelming. Colourful promoters flyering for their shows, theatrical obscure actors dancing like worms on the cobbled streets to be noticed, clowns, comedians, street performers, singers, dancers, film directors, actors with literally hundreds of shows were on offer to see. Everyone did anything they could to stand out from the rest. Flags, posters, people in costumes, my eyes were filled to the brim with eccentricity and the freedom from people being able to express themselves in so many ways.

I was only in the beautiful city for ten days, so I wanted to experience as much as I could. It was so cultured and historic. After performing two open spots a day, I went and walked alone at night, finding old narrow cobbled alleyways and curious uneven walkways with dimly lit street lamps, and steep stone steps that could have led me anywhere. During my time there, I met other comics new and old from around the world, and went to see as much comedy as I could. This gave me some real insight to what it would be like to have my own show up there. One of the shows I stumbled upon purely by accident, was a sketch group called Four Screws Loose. I wouldn't have usually stayed to watch, as sketch groups never really caught my attention, but I noticed these four guys on stage, in the middle of singing and dancing to a boy band song, but completely taking the piss. Exaggerated thrusts and over the top moves really made me laugh. Physical and visual comedy was what I had always loved. The facial expressions I pulled on stage while I told my stories on stage always bought me good reactions. In such a short amount of time, I had a crash course in comedy. Meeting new people, hearing their comedy experiences, adapting to all the different audiences I performed to, and understanding all the work that went into each show. It was intense and tiring. But I loved every moment and as soon as I returned to London, I started to think about a show of my own.

Diary Extract – September 16, 2011

Hello, I'm Naomi Hefter, and I'm a wallower! Edinburgh Festival was over, and I was on a major emotional comedown from such an amazing experience. But it appears there are more of us wallowers around than I thought! Whether you are a comedian, a fashion designer, or firefighter or a teacher, whatever you are, SOME people can't help but have a good old wallow. However, when I told my logical straightforward social worker housemate about this secret 'hobby' of mine, she couldn't help but laugh out loud. "So, you just sit there, in your bed, play a sad song and cry away?" she asked me. Yes! OK, so scrolling through my songs, trying to find REM's Everybody Hurts amongst so many Ibiza trance tracks can be a small hindrance. But once the music starts, the tears just flow, and the painful thoughts in my head get more vivid by the tear. But what IS wallowing I ask myself! Thinking about all the bad things that have happened to you in the past? Worrying about things that haven't even happened in the future? Or just feeling sorry for yourself because you are having a bit of an 'off' day? Personally, I think it's a simple case of crying in your own narcissistic self-pity and not bothering to tell yourself to get a grip. That's why so many of us comedians do it. I've had many conversations, with various comics, who have confessed to having their moments of wallowing self-indulgence. Apparently, the unhappier you are, the more likely you are to try and make others laugh. So, it suddenly all makes sense! I've even been asked how often I do it! (Wallow, that is) So I thought... Once a week? No, surely, I don't spend once a week sitting in my bed, alone, crying to myself, do I? Last Thursday I was wallowing, and I looked at myself in the mirror while I was doing it. This only made me wallow more. As I looked upon the puffed up, crinkled face of a single, struggling comedian, wallowing in her own pathetic misery. But then I quickly became wise and thought, it's actually very healthy to have a good wallow. It cleanses the soul, releases all the pain and sadness built up inside. It's kind of like an orgasm of built up emotions, where you feel so much better after. So, I carried on wallowing for the rest of the night! I woke up feeling refreshed, vitalised, and stronger than I had in a week! I've just updated my CV—Hobbies: Theatre, writing, badminton and wallowing.

So, for any logical people out there reading this, who might think its cringe worthy, time wasting and pathetic to wallow, give it a go! It may become your new favourite thing to do!

When I was physically and mentally back in the real world of London, September, October, November and December was a life of working for the tax advisors, gigging, and going out with Povs now we had met. I had the odd text from David from time to time, which always stung as we still weren't back together. But I was the fool who loved him so much and was always happy to hear from him so replied with open arms.

Another December had rather quickly appeared uninvited. 'Twas the season to be jolly, but I wasn't. Povs was back in New York and I felt that trepidation of loneliness loom over me again. The tax advisor's job wanted me to wear a Christmas jumper to get into the spirit, which I was not willing to participate in. I didn't care much for Christmas, and I didn't care that colleagues and friends called me The Grinch. I missed enjoying spending money on loved ones. Every year, there was one person I missed, and one person was missing from my life; David. On Christmas day itself, back in Cheltenham, I had a better time than previous years. My mother, brother and sister and I were all together, and we all slept in till 11 am. Waking up with a glass of Bucks fizz before exchanging and opening gifts. We never had the traditional Christmas food or pudding. Instead, a steak followed with a variety of cheese. We drank Hazelnut Baileys whilst watching the EastEnders Special. Three days in and I was ready to go back to London. It was just long enough before my mother began to bring up the past. It had caused so many blazing arguments and that Christmas had been a good one for the first time in years, so I wanted to leave that chat.

Before I knew it, it was New Year's Eve, and Povs was back from America and we had arranged a huge night out to celebrate the New Year in. It was a freezing cold night and we were dressed in ridiculous costumes that had no connection or theme to each other's outfit. Povs decided to be dressed in a corset, skirt and wearing a volumised black and red wig with devil horns, called herself a sexy secretary. Me, I was dressed in a sailor's uniform. I loved wearing bright red lipstick and the little white sailor hat, with a sequined anchor sewn on the front. I felt naughty and nautical. We ended up in the huge gay club Heaven, which was placed right behind The Strand. We had a ball. A foam party began and was flying everywhere, glitter and confetti filled the club at midnight, and laughter filled the room while drinks went down a treat.

At exactly midnight, a text from David buzzed through informing me he didn't wish to see me again and wanted to move on with his life. I was having such a good time, but I felt my heart sink underneath what seemed to be apt with my sailor costume on. It hurt whenever I thought about David. I missed him every single day. I missed his hugs, I missed us dancing together, I missed the intense chemistry we had, I even missed the way he rubbed my arms when he hugged me goodnight. But with the company I was in and with the atmosphere around me, I felt good. And knowing 2012 would be so much fun with Povs, I didn't cry. On the outside, no one would have thought or known that deep down I still cared so much.

2012

The Dating Game

January was not just a month of rubbish weather and dieting for most, it was also the month where the majority of mere mortals were completely broke. Even though I had been temping at the tax firm for a few months, I woke up on January 1 with a fridge of crabsticks, and my cupboard full of Super Noodles. Living in London and temping was hard. Rent was expensive, and I had no savings. I started to think about how to make some money from nothing. I wasn't prepared to sell my body for sex, so I looked up how much I could get for selling my eggs. But I didn't know a lot about the field of egg selling and considering I wasn't sure if I wanted my own children, I didn't think I was the right candidate to start selling the one thing that produced kids. Then I thought about selling my knickers, I had heard there was a huge market for plenty of people online with odd fetishes who were willing to pay a large wad of cash for girl's dirty pants. So, I did some research. I found some worn underwear on eBay that were selling for £2.99. It just wasn't worth it. The postage alone would cost more than what I could make.

Living with two new flatmates, who couldn't be further apart in personality was a new chapter in my life. If I had known what I was letting myself in for, I would have taken the risk and carried on looking for different people. I was delighted that I was given the freedom by the landlord to choose who I wanted to live with as I had been there three years already. I didn't mind what sex the new tenants were, what they did for a living, or who they were as long as they were decent human beings.

One person who came to view the flat was James, a stocky, bearded, quirky looking guy wearing a Hawaiian shirt who worked in the media. I was instantly attracted to him as he wandered around the flat. It appeared he was attracted to me also because after two hours of chatting away like old friends, he suddenly kissed me which led to us kissing franticly against the wall in the hall. A kiss was all it was, and two days later, James declined the flat, explaining living with me would only be complicated. I never saw him again.

The first to move in was a 6'4" blonde man from Belgium, called Ewald. At first, he appeared to be a polite and decent person. But look up the word ANAL in the dictionary and you would see his face. He was out of bed at 5 am to work out, he cooked nothing but organic food from scratch every single evening. He never drank alcohol and he read books on ancient architecture. On paper, he had the attributes to be the perfect boyfriend or husband, if he let his hair down occasionally. To live with on the other hand, he was a different story. Controlling and interfering, like a nosy dad. Sure, it was great to have Mr Anal always cleaning and dusting, and polishing the flat every time I came home, but I was also unable to find my shoes, my bathroom toiletries, or any of my clean clothes. I often found my wet clean clothes that were left on the clothes horse to dry, folded up on my bed, which left me a wet patch to sleep on and my clean clothes now smelling of damp. Moving around my wet clothes was one thing, but to go into my bedroom without asking was another. On several occasions, I found my shampoo and face wash was also left in my bedroom too, just so there were no ring marks from the bottles left on the corner of the bath. My shoes would disappear into thin air when I came home and took them off near the door, he had gone into my room again and put them under my bed. This sent my blood rocketing, considering I had told him time and time again that he couldn't just go marching into my bedroom whenever he felt like it. For me, what topped it off was when he went through the magazine rack and threw away my collection of special edition magazines, I owned on various artists which I had for years. Within the same week, he had moved my drying clothes yet again from the clotheshorse and this time put them on the radiator, causing one of my dresses to shrink to the size of a baby's t-shirt. He was a nightmare.

Imagine the absolute opposite who had moved in three days after Ewald. His name was Paul. A man who claimed he was a walking knowledge of house music. He was from Liverpool but had lived in Birmingham for the past five years, so had a slightly muddled accent. If you looked up the word INCONSIDERATE in the dictionary, there you would find Paul's face. Unable to open his own bedroom door, it was that cluttered. Every morning, his beard trimmings and spat out toothpaste would be left in the sink for me to find, and he was my human alarm clock. A pattern started to form within weeks of him moving in, when he would stumble in at 4 am on Wednesdays, Thursdays, Fridays and Saturdays, slamming the heavy front door every time. This woke me up like a startled rabbit hearing a gunfire. He would then bellow on the phone, instead of talk or whisper, and start cooking eggs and bacon, banging and crashing while doing so. Inconsiderate, selfish, rude and lazy. After weeks of the same thing, I had a saved text message that was sent to him at precisely 4:30am four times a week. The text message in capitals read, SHUT THE FUCK UP. It got so bad that one night I came out of my bedroom, threatening him that a person called Vincent, who I made up on the spot was going to come around, hold Paul down and sew his mouth up if he didn't SHUT THE FUCK UP. The being woken up part didn't really bother me; it was being kept awake with his noise that really stressed me out. Every time Povs would come over, she took the piss out of both of them calling Ewald 'Egaw' accidentally-on-purpose, and would offer Paul wet wipes to clean up his mess and a microphone for us to hear him even more.

During my time still working for the tax advisors, I had an informal interview with a guy I had met on the comedy circuit, who worked for the online newspaper, The Huffington Post where I had the chance to write blogs for them. It would be for free, but it was a chance to showcase my writing. After sending over some work to him, and being told to change a few bits here and there, I started to send over monthly blogs which I really enjoyed. As I typed away blog and article ideas at work, my presence at the tax firm was hanging by a thread. I had already received several verbal warnings for my extremely hyperactive, outrageous and unpredictable behaviour, plus a written warning for telling one of my colleagues his trousers looked too tight around his todger. So that June, just eighteen months working there, I received a letter informing me I had been fired. And rightly so. It was a story I would use in my comedy performances for years to come. I was caught waxing my vagina at my desk. I was bored what can I say. And after receiving a free waxing strip in a magazine one day, I decided to try it out. With my legs already smooth and I wasn't prepared to wax my arms or eyebrows, so trying it out on my over grown landing strip of pubic hair was the only option. I was wearing a skirt, so managed to wiggle down my underwear and place the strip on the area I had been neglecting. When looking at me behind my desk, no one would have known a thing about what was going on from the waist down. I suddenly realised, I had never once in my life, waxed any part of my body before. So, I googled how to use it, and there it said to rub the strip until warm and place the strip on the hair. Google told me that once the strip was placed, I was to rip it off very fast towards me. I did. But nothing happened. I was expecting excruciating pain as I had seen in the films, nothing; except that the wax had left the paper strip and was now congealed within my pubic region. It was a mess; it looked as though I had rubbed bright pink, chewed up, wet bubble gum all over my vagina. I didn't know what to do. I stared for a while, considering my actions. Just as I started to pull my knickers up, the female head tax advisor walked by and saw everything. Luckily for me, she found it amusing, and got me into her office and handed me some scissors.

"You are going to have to cut out that clumped hair," she said in a somewhat understanding tone. She handed me the scissors to cut away the sticky mess from between my legs. I braced myself, ready to cut off one hard lump of hair as close to the skin as possible. It was then the CEO walked right past her office and saw us. There was no going back. I knew at that very moment, when I saw the look on his stern 73-year-old face, I was a goner. I appealed just in case I could win my job back, but if I was being completely honest with myself, I didn't really want to be there anyway. I had no passion for answering the phone and I had no interest in tax. Povs came with me to the meeting and acted as my witness. We tried out very best not to burst out laughing as the CEO read out my letter of dismissal. Povs held her nose as he read out the words 'for placing a waxing strip along your vagina' in his serious monotone manner. I knew I had no chance in getting my job back, but at least I tried. As much as I didn't like to be out of work again, Povs and I found that moment hilarious.

As fate and a little bit of luck came into play, my job situation and its timing was on my side. I had been on a particularly bad date, with a comic who considered himself as the new, funnier version of Jude Law; which wasn't the case. The date was pretty disastrous. I was being fed lines about the next dates and how much he liked me. But I saw right through the cliché lies that all he wanted was a shag. But one thing I did have to thank him for was that he got me into a competition he was hosting, which I hadn't heard about on the circuit. This competition opened a few new doors for me.

Two days later, when Monday mornings were usually days of either sitting in a boring office, or looking to work in one, I turned up to join a large queue of comedians. There, I was entered into the competition by my 'one-date Jude Law wannabe'. The competition was called The Jongleur's Comic Idol Competition. I felt a little out of my depth, considering so many established acts were waiting in the queue. The competition was being held because Jongleurs Comedy Club were looking for new talent. I recognised a few other comedians I had gigged with around London. Other known and unknown acts had travelled from other parts of the country to be there too, so all in all, there were about 150 acts hungry to perform and get through the next stage. I didn't know a lot about Jongleurs as a business, apart from seeing a famous line-up of acts on boards outside clubs around London.

The judges enjoyed my look and my set during my first audition, telling me I was marketable and could be used for TV work. Things were going great and after a long day waiting around, going through each comedian, I was told I was through to the quarterfinals.

Two weeks later, with more auditions to get through, I had made it to the finals and I was ecstatic. Twelve of us were left to perform in the final, with the winner getting onto the books of Jongleurs and given regular paid gigs around the country. As the same line-up of judges had seen my set a few times though the competition, I had made the catastrophic mistake to try brand new untested material in the final. As each joke exited my lips with not many laughs to follow, I knew then I had done something incredibly stupid. I never made that mistake again.

As much as I wanted to put the terrible gig I had done in the finals behind me, I had received an email from Loaded Magazine who had previously published some of my jokes in earlier issues. The editor contacted me personally and asked for me to do a seven-page photo shoot for them with an interview about stand-up comedy. Of course, I jumped at the chance.

The shoot went brilliantly with gorgeous shots. As I was asked questions about when and how I started comedy, I felt this was a real chance that I could get my name out there.

Two weeks later, Povs and I headed to W H Smith, and bought three issues of the magazine and fell to the pages where I was featured. Seven entire pages all about little old Naomi. It was so brilliant to see, and my interview hadn't been twisted or changed in any way. I felt I needed to tell David about my shoot as I was excited and proud, plus I wanted him to see the photos for them to possibly make him miss me. He replied the next day, and told me he had bought a copy and was thinking of me but couldn't see me as he had started to date someone. The wind was knocked out of me as the tears ran down my cheeks as the words from his text started to blur. All I could do was focus on what Povs and I were about to embark on, we were off on a road trip to Edinburgh festival.

The road trip with Povs alone was a riot, and once we arrived, we had just over two weeks performing half an hour each during our 3pm slot every day. For two female comedians, doing their first double hander at the biggest comedy festival in the world, felt like we were back in our first semester at university all over again, ready to soak in a lot of knowledge in the world of comedy. As Povs and I got to our venue at The Three Sisters on Cowgate, we laughed as we gazed upon where we would be performing our show. Outside the pub stood a static double decker bus all kitted out ready for shows to be performed. As we walked up the narrow bus staircase, I was wearing a pair of high heels, and a short stripy blue and white dress. When I reached the top of the bus, I quickly discovered I was far too tall to stand up straight. My head hit the ceiling and my neck was crooked as I stooped uncomfortably to fit. Povs, on the other hand, a good nine inches shorter than me stood comfortably in her red Converse trainers. There was only one thing for it. I had to buy some flat practical shoes to wear. They had to be comfy and something that would last. Fuck it, I decided to buy my first pair of Converse trainers. If someone had told me five years prior to that moment, that I would be performing on a double decker bus wearing a pair of Converse trainers, I would have told them they were definitely not talking about me. But there I was, a new pair of white canvas trainers on my feet. I was surprisingly fond of them. Each day Povs and I performed our show, we got better and better. Roaring laughs at my unexpected punch lines, quick banter and adlibs with a variety of audience members who sat close by on the bus seats. It was only then during my time in Edinburgh I got that light bulb moment every comedian waits for. It's a significant time in any performer's career, when you have been experimenting with different aspects of yourself and you're waiting for a moment when stand up suddenly becomes so much easier. Once I had bought those Converse, something about my presence, my delivery and body language completely changed. I was relaxed, I was comfortable, I was fluid with my movements, and mostly, I had become more relatable and my stories fit with the persona I held. The light bulb moment had opened my mind up and I was suddenly performing great gigs every time I went on stage.

And just like the first month I experienced at university, one-week alone into Edinburgh festival, I felt exactly the same. I was tired, bloated and living off adrenaline and the roller coaster ride of emotions. My new white Converse were ruined from plenty of drink spillage and muddy rain, but I was loving every minute of it. I was sure I had given myself IBS after eating nothing but cheese and onion pasties, Big Macs and a few too many very large German sausages that were sold on the street market stools. However, knowing I had a show to do each day with Povs, made that experience one of the best times of my life.

Shoplifting smoked salmon to keep me fed was in my past and as much as I was frequently in and out of work, I could at least afford to feed myself. However, over the years, shoplifting was still something I turned to when I felt overwhelmed by any sadness or anger. Shoplifting still gave me that quick fix and that buzz that suppressed my negative feelings momentarily. It was also a bad habit I had gotten myself into that I was really trying to break. So right in the middle of my time in Edinburgh, after a row I had with a comedian who came onto the bus drunk while I was performing my set and ruined our show that afternoon, when standing in the middle of Boots with Povs waiting outside, I found myself shoplifting some AA batteries I didn't even need. And right outside the shop, I was caught. An undercover security guard approached me outside to find the batteries firmly in the palm of my hand. It turned out, Scottish security guards are a little harsher than English ones, and instead of being banned from the shop, the police were called, and I was taken to the cells. As Povs watched me being driven away in the back of a police car, she caught the bus to the police station to see me there while I took a statement. As I lost my dignity, all that was on my mind while I politely cooperated was that we had a show to do in 40 minutes' time. My thoughts were startled as two police men suddenly marched through the station doors, holding up a man who looked as though had passed out on heroin. With his feet dragging behind him, I suddenly wanted to just get out of there. Once I was free to go, I was so embarrassed and ashamed I wasn't in the mood at all to do my usual set. Instead, I decided to discuss what had happened to me less than an hour before. Surprisingly, just standing there in front of the audience, rifting off my experience had the crowd in stitches and many of the audience members asked me afterwards if what had happened was true, which for a change, I didn't mind.

That night as I lay in bed, I couldn't fall asleep as the day's episode ran through my head over and over. It was only then I decided to do some research on stealing and discovered I might have suffered from a condition called Kleptomania.

Kleptomania is a condition characterised by the irresistible urge to steal. He or she will steal items they do not need or that have little money or value. Kleptomania often emerges sometime during adolescence and appears more commonly with woman than men. People with this condition experience a build-up of tension before the theft, and a consequent release of anxiety and tension when committing a theft. Stealing results in feelings of gratification relief and even pleasure while the theft may relieve the tension the individual is experiencing, he or she may be left with the feeling of guilt, remorse and shame.

It is important to understand that kleptomanias do not steal for their own personal gain; they are not stealing based on a financial gain.

Two days before we were heading back to London, on a night out with Povs and some fellow comics we had met, I received a text. It was David, who, the last time I heard from had told me I wouldn't hear from him again as he had met someone else. His latest text told me he couldn't stop thinking about me. I remember Povs' face like a photograph when I showed her his message. She was furious. I only felt relief. Relief that the plan he had made to let me go had gone out the window.

With the blink of an eye, it was October, and I was standing in front of two cameras, introducing a new TV show. I was offered the job as a new TV presenter for a show on Sky after I had been spotted from my Loaded Magazine shoot. The new TV show had the same premise and setup of Dragons Den. But instead of new entrepreneurs, there would be new entertainers. Each entertainer would stand in front of a row of four celebrity panellists to show their skill or talent. They were then received feedback suggesting what or where they could go with their ideas, or they were to be told how terrible and untalented they were. I had never considered presenting, but I enjoyed reading cue cards and using my cheeky banter to chat to each contestant. Even with the headache from the bright lights and wearing four layers of thick foundation on my face, the sweaty armpits and a stomach full of butterflies, I was feeling so happy to be out of the office environment and doing something creative and worthwhile with my time.

The director and owner of this new show and business was as eccentric as they come. His electric blue, crushed velvet suit from the 1960s and his pipe smoking away as it hung out of his mouth. At first, I felt at home, I felt I was mixing with my kind of people. But as time went by, I noticed things were a bit… dodgy. Outside the studio, there were little huts scattered around, and I would sometimes spot naked girls walking into them. I never once questioned who they were or what was happening, but I kept it in the back of my mind and carried on filming for the show as normal.

It started off with a rumour. The rumour was that the director and owner of the show was a porn star. I also heard he kept other porn stars hidden around the studios. Some of the crew had thought it had been going on for a while, but there was no real proof of anything. The naked girls popped in my head, but I was unable to imagine that such an outrageous rumour could be true. So, the very next day, after a long day filming four episodes of the TV show, I went home and put on YouPorn to help me out with some burning questions. It was a chilly Friday night and I lay in bed with a bowl of Super Noodles. Lo and behold, when typing in the name of the man who gave me my presenting job, I suddenly saw the thumbnail of his face on my computer screen. I clicked on the clip and saw his wrinkled-up face having sex on a dentist's chair. I was too shocked, sickened, intrigued and morbidly curious to look away. I kept on watching while I ate my noodles, not taking my eyes off the screen all the while spilling noodle juice down my chin. Once the 12-minute clip finished, I turned off my laptop and watched Disney's Sleeping Beauty to make myself feel innocent again.

We filmed two series of the show and it wasn't much of a hit. The panellists were old school radio and TV stars from the 80s, so no one under the age of thirty watching or auditioning, knew who they were. Things were beginning to fizzle out like cheap fireworks and soon enough, everyone knew out about the porn star boss. I had decided to leave the job once I had made the discovery of how seedy and shady it was.

Suddenly, for the first time in my life, after months of paid gigs, TV work and magazine and newspaper exposure, I didn't have to panic about paying the rent. However, I learnt that money definitely couldn't buy happiness. Walking into Selfridges and buying myself a pair of Christian Louboutin heels, just because I could, felt nice. But I was still alone, and all I could think about was David and wished he was by my side.

I lost count how many times I had been on a crappy first date with some guy I had met, trying to move on from David. When arranging a date, those who knew I did stand-up comedy, automatically assumed I only wanted a date with the guy just to get some juicy stories to add to my comedy set. Words failed me when I tried to explain how frustrating that was. Had it not occurred to these people that I was on a date because I was looking for love, or simultaneously, looking to fall out of love with David and move on? I flirted with the idea of meeting new people from an online dating site. I thought it might help distract me from David, considering nothing was happening from his end. Once I joined a dating site and uploaded my photos, opening each message and reading that 90% of the men were just asking for a shag, not only left me feeling drained, but ironically, left me feeling even more lonely. All I had asked for was a gentleman who owned a full head of hair, aged between 25 and 37 and had a kind face. I was not expecting to be bombarded with messages from bald 45-year-old men looking for a shag. I ended up going on a few dates before closing my account. All of which were so bad, I was left feeling frustrated and tired. Before closing the account, I asked myself, *Would I have approached any of these men on a night out?* The answer was no. After the dates, I had enough of forcing love, so I left it to find out what was to come the natural way. Some of the dates from the site were more memorable than others. After each date I experienced, I kept a diary of my dating disasters as a memory to possibly smile about one day. And I never spoke about any of those dates in my comedy sets.

My Dating Diary
Mute Guy

The first date from the site I had joined I was feeling optimistic. I lost an hour of my life forever as I sat with this guy who had the charisma of a snail. Actually, snails can be quite charming, this guy had the charisma of a slug. A dead one. I would rather have spent that hour watching snails racing in slow motion. Meeting on a Sunday afternoon in a pub on Embankment for a roast seemed like the perfect setting to a first date. But after fifty minutes of me busting my balls, trying to get him to give me answers other than yes and no, I had given up. Half way through my overpriced leg of chicken with veg, I kindly told him this wasn't working, I shook his hand, wished him luck and left. The only regret I have from that date was that I didn't ask to take the rest of my chicken and roast potatoes home with me in a doggie bag.

Tom Cruise Guy

Meeting him in a bar in the city, we got on well over our chat that he could easily have been the identical lost twin of Tom Cruise. Not really my type physically but still, a novel date to go on. It was the perfect date until strangers thought he really was Tom Cruise, and when asking him for a photo he actually put on a Tom Cruise voice and pretended to be him. He was from Northampton and the Tom Cruise impersonation was horrendous. I didn't ask him for an autograph or anything else for that matter after that.

Naked Guy

This was the date that cooked me dinner at his place, something I wouldn't usually do on a first date, but we got on really well and had been exchanging texts too. Then after a little kiss on the sofa, he decided to show me 'the tattoo' on his arse, but instead, just got his penis out which was fully erect. He stood there, trousers around his ankles with his arms spread-eagled out like Jesus on the cross and said, "I just wanted to show you what I've got," looking very pleased with himself. I quickly made my excuses and left.

Tiny Hands Guy

When you love someone, him having tiny hands shouldn't and doesn't matter. When you love someone, all their imperfections become perfections and all the compromises you have to make didn't matter for the relationship to work. But when you are on a first date and the chemistry isn't there, tiny hands are enough to put you off for life.

Out of Date Photo Guy

This was my last and final date from the dating website. Purely because I was now just exhausted and depressed with it all. They had all been disasters and this one was just as bad. His photo on the site was about 10 years out of date! Not only did I not recognise him when he showed up, but his tits were bigger than mine. I sat and had a drink with him, and as the beads of sweat dripped down his forehead into his pint, I wondered if this was my life. Yes, it really was.

I had been dreading December. Povs's visa had run out and she was being deported back to the States. I had surprised her with a letter I had received from the Prime minister's secretary. I had secretly written to David Cameron asking him if Povs could stay in England as he was a hard-working citizen, and I would be lost without her. Unfortunately, David Cameron had more important things on his plate. She cried and laughed when I showed her the letter and response. In return, Povs had a gift for me which she gave me at her leaving party. A book of famous written love letters and poetry. One of which she circled that was recited from Sex and the city, the movie. I had loved the words and she had remembered.

Though still in bed, my thoughts go out to you, my Immortal Beloved, now and then joyfully, then sadly, waiting to learn whether or not fate will hear us—I can live only wholly with you or not at all—Yes, I am resolved to wander so long away from you until I can fly to your arms and say that I am really at home with you, and can send my soul enwrapped in you into the land of spirits—Yes, unhappily it must be so—You will be the more contained since you know my fidelity to you. No one else can ever possess my heart—never—never—oh God, why must one be parted from one whom one so loves. And yet my life in V[ienna] is now a wretched life—Your love makes me at once the happiest and the unhappiest of men—At my age, I need a steady, quiet life—can that be so in our connection? My angel, I have just been told that the mail coach goes every day— therefore, I must close at once so that you may receive the letter at once—Be calm, only by a clam consideration of our existence can we achieve our purpose to live together—Be calm—love me—today—yesterday—what tearful longings for you—you—you—my life—my all—farewell. Oh, continue to love me—never misjudge the most faithful heart of your beloved. Ever thine, ever mine, ever ours. – 'Immortal Beloved'

Letter, July 7, 1812 – Ludwig Van Beethoven.

2013

Whirlwind

Waking up in January 2013 wasn't fun. Povs had gone back to America and I hadn't heard from David since October. But then again, there had been a pattern of hearing from David every January. It was the first weekend in, and I was feeling so unwell with what felt like the flu. The battery on my phone had died and I really didn't care. It had been off for at least 24 hours when I suddenly had an overwhelming feeling that David had messaged me. I found some motivation to plug in my phone, and there, five minutes before I charged my battery when I got that feeling, he had made contact. It had been three long months, and it was him asking how I was and if I fancied a drink. I didn't feel overly happy by the message, I wasn't angry, I wasn't even surprised, I knew I would hear from him again.

A week later, I may have been out of work, but I still had enough money from the presenting job to support myself. I wondered what I could do with some of the money, so I started with setting up a direct debit to help tigers. They were a huge passion of mine and the idea of tigers not existing on the planet was unthinkable Secondly, there was no time like the present, I booked a flight to Chicago to visit Povs. She was so excited when I told her I would be there in under ten weeks' time. I decided to text David there and then. I wanted him to know when I would be going and that I would possibly move there if I liked the city. I had no intention of moving to America, but something made me want to give him a jolt up the arse to make him think. I was never one for playing games, but it had come to a point where he needed to know I was doing things without him, as much as it pained me.

Knowing I was finally going to see America for the first time was such an exciting feeling. It took me thirty years to get there, and I was finally going. I had started counting down the days at 100 and was packing on day 50.

The day finally came, March 13th and I was off to America. David kindly took me to the airport, helping me with my suitcase. After realising I had taken us to the wrong terminal at Heathrow, there was a panic as David quickly got us a taxi to head to the correct terminal. David shook his head and laughed at how bad my travelling alone skills were. Just as I left to check in, David handed me a card as we were saying our goodbyes. He told me to read it on the plane. Of course, I couldn't wait until the plane, I opened the card as soon as David was out of sight.

Dear Nay,
I hope you have a wonderful time in Chicago and enjoy your time there. Let me know you have arrived safe.

David
Xxxx
Xx
x

Eight hours and 30 minutes later, I was in the windy city of Chicago. I was so happy to see Povs again and it was like we had only seen each other the day before. Povs was excited to show me around American shops, to give me an idea of how over the top her country really was. We ventured to a 'grocery store', to view the continuous isles of sugar-filled jars of maple syrup and endless rows of cheese filled cans. I had never seen anything like it. It reminded me of something out of a pop art poster. I was also looking at ten heart attacks as I read the ingredients and saw things I had never heard of in those cans of creamy processed whipped cheese. On nights out, I couldn't quite get over how confident the American men were either. Confident but not arrogant, compliments without the clichés. I felt completely at ease as there were real gentlemen in America. No groping, gawping, grabbing, drooling, staring, squeezing, fondling, feeling, or perving on women to make them feel uncomfortable. Chicago just wasn't like that. I was really enjoying the culture change.

I performed four comedy gigs whilst I stayed in Chicago with Povs. I was nervous about how the American audience would take me. But I received great reactions and responses from the crowds. No chauvinism or sexism. No drunken heckles or slurring jibes. Just laughter and smiles with the added bonus of being told how much they loved the British accent. A chap approached me after one gig, speaking in an extremely strong Chicago accent, "Girrrl, you fine, even more than Alicia Keys, can I have your autograph?" Of course, I happily signed my name on a business card before Povs and I headed to The Matchbox bar, famous for being the smallest bar in Chicago. It was so narrow, people had to walk through it sideways.

David had left me several emails while I was away, checking how much I was enjoying Chicago. I knew telling him I would possibly move there could give him the jolt that he needed, so I didn't regret telling him that white lie. People really do want what they can't have, it seems. I waited a few days after I returned to contact him, which was extremely hard for me.

Diary Extract – March 20, 2013

Traveling back to London, I woke up on the plane to hear a little boy ask his father, "What did you want to be when you grow up, Daddy?" and the 40-something-year-old man replied, "I want to be in a band." That response made me smile. His 'wants' instead of 'wanted' made me think. It doesn't matter what age someone is; people can still dream, people can still pursue, and anyone can follow their heart and be who they want to be if they just put fears aside. When I grow up, I want to be recognised for my work, inspire people with mental health issues, be married to David and to just be happy. I still question what this is all about. Life, I mean. Why we choose certain paths. Is everyone we meet for a reason, or is it one big random jumble of coincidence? Being, or even just feeling accepted by strangers, short-term acquaintances, potential lovers, seems so important. But I can't help but wonder, when I'm 85, sitting in my mansion like Mrs Havisham, sipping on my vodka martini smelling of cat's piss, am I really going to care about being accepted by people who were passing moments that meant nothing to me? Probably not. So why did I constantly feel the need to explain myself to people and receive recognition for the choices I make. Perhaps it's all down to love. At the end of the day, that's what we are here for. That's what life is all about when you really think about it. Feeling accepted is only part of society. Most people, especially in the creative world, who are trying to expressive themselves, need to feel that understanding from anyone willing to look or listen. But at the end of the day, the beauty is, every single person, no matter who they are, is simply looking for someone to love and be loved in return.

It was Samar's 30th birthday party towards the end of March. This was a girl that had a love for beautiful makeup, good music and anything Disney. So, of course, she combined the three for her celebrations. Except I didn't get the memo about the Disney part. She had hired a little place in Kings Cross called Drink Shop & Do, and I was surprised I had never heard of the place, considering I only lived up the road. It was a quirky little shop, upstairs selling cupcakes, and independent stationary and retro sweets. Downstairs was a completely different story: once a brothel, turned nightclub. Huge neon red lights screamed SEX as you walked down into the basement, to be greeted with a fun bar that played funky music and served strong beautifully made cocktails. I turned up to see a large group of people I didn't know, all dressed in Disney characters. Samar, looking the way she does with her thick long black hair and tanned skin, was destined to be dressed as Princess Jasmin, but to my surprise was dressed as Cinderella. Meeting Samar's friends, dancing and having fun, I noticed the DJ playing some classic songs, David Bowie's *Let's Dance*, Eurythmic's *Sweet Dreams*, Blondies *Atomic* and many retro funky tunes that always got me dancing. There was something intriguing about the DJ. With his tall lanky exterior and black hair, he wasn't my type physically, but he played music as though he was inside each song, feeling the music whilst having an air of mystery to him. I found myself approaching him and handing over my number.

Before I knew, it was my turn to turn the big 3 0! On the one tragic, inevitable day of my life. I had approximately 18,220 days left to live, and in some professions, I was now past it. However, I was still asked for ID and I didn't feel or look 30. I remember being ten years old and thinking thirty was ancient. Didn't being thirty mean a mortgage, a husband and 2.4 children, with a red Nissan in the driveway? But even though I thought that was what happened at 30, they were things I never desired. And I couldn't have been further away from that 'grown up' life so many people chose to have. I was informed by people older than 35 that the decade of our 30s was meant to be the best ten years of our lives. I hoped that those old folks were right, because my twenties were had been hard. Losing the love of my life, moving from place to place, learning some valuable lessons and making some huge mistakes.

I decided to book the same venue as Samar. Drink, Shop & Do in Kings Cross. Not only was it free, but I had kept in touch with Jamie, the DJ there, and really enjoyed the music he played. To this day, David Bowie's *Let's Dance* still reminds me of that venue.

I invited everyone I knew in London, which was a fair amount by then. Comedians, promoters, housemates and many, many, many, many people I had worked with from the endless jobs I had done across London. David was on a stag do in Scotland, but he had sent me a message that morning hoping I have a great night. And I did have a lovely night, but having different groups of friends, comedians, work mates, girls I had met through other girls, and housemates, they all kept in their own little circles in the venue. I felt like I was at my wedding, milling around to each group, checking to make sure they were having a good time. Once I stopped bothering everyone and made the decision to just have a good time myself, I let my hair down and danced the night away with a row of drinks waiting for me that people had bought. Of course, Povs not being there felt weird, it was never quite the same without her. We joked that I would take my laptop to the venue and have it on in the middle of the room while we she was on Skype.

When I finally got home, merry and happy from the outcome of the evening, Jamie messaged me saying he had got a taxi and was sitting outside my flat and wanted to come in to see me. There was something very intriguing and mischievous about him. But knowing that David and I were a little more in contact with our messages, I said no to Jamie coming up.

Over the next few days, Jamie kept contacting me and asked to come and see my gig. I had just finished a temp job for the fashion label Lacoste, just off Oxford Street where the people were nice, friendly and down to earth for a change. It was a place where I actually didn't get fired from or walked out on, so once the job was finished, I was free to spend some time with Jamie, but I made it clear it would only be as friends. And after all, he was a DJ who worked nights, so being free during the day for a while, it was good to spend time with someone until I found my next job.

We met up on Brick Lane, a few hours before I had a gig at Dirty Dick's on Bishopsgate. Jamie had a cool calm exterior about him, which almost made him slightly intimidating. I was used to men who were either shy and nervous, or extroverted and cocky, the two types were especially prominent around the comedy scene. Jamie was also a bad boy, a type I was never interested in. He had spent time in prison and now he was keeping his nose clean with DJing. Over the next few days and weeks, we started to spend a lot more time together. He would come along to see my gigs, and I would go to the bars he played at and got to know his friends, and often end at his place after a night out for a house party. Huge DJ decks filled his living room floor inside his flat on Brick lane, and before I knew it, it was turning into a whirlwind of madness. I was starting to really like this person, but I knew I had no future with him. We were too different, and like every time I met someone new, David's sixth sense kicked in and he wanted to see me again. I couldn't say no. David was my drug.

I was still out of work by the end of June and my money situation was back to normal, with me not having much of it. My life was gigging most nights, writing and preparing for my first solo show for the Edinburgh Festival. I was also sorting out the last few pieces on the agenda, booking my preview show in London, having my posters and flyers made, and promoting and marketing myself. It was just a month before heading to Edinburgh when I spotted something on Facebook that had quite an effect on my life. A comedy promoter had written a status on Facebook, simply saying the words, "If you are female, single and in your late twenties or early thirties, email this woman." I was all of those things. I had no idea what it was for, but I went ahead and emailed her.

Her name was Juliet and she was a TV producer for Channel 4, putting together a documentary about single people living in London, and the reasons behind why so many people are still, in fact, single at a certain age. When I told her my situation, she was keen to meet me for a coffee.

When I met Juliet, she reminded me of Alexa Chung, natural, slim and very chic. Well spoken, dressed in nautical-style clothing. She asked me some questions over coffee and explained more about the idea of the programme. It would be filmed in a documentary style, about one man and one woman who don't know each other and would go on a quest to find out why that other person might still be single. This would involve meeting that person's friends, family members and even their ex-partners. I was certainly interested, but I knew in my mind the only ex I needed for this show probably wouldn't do it. I didn't think for one minute I would be chosen for the show anyway.

I was called into her office the following week and was told to do something a little different. I was asked to not prepare anything, which left me feeling out of my comfort zone. Maybe that was the point. So, when I arrived, along with many others who had come for the same reason, I was asked to do anything I wanted in front of the camera. Absolutely anything. So, I decided right there and then to recite my comedy poem, *The Bitterness of Singleton City*, which left her amused and surprised.

"Where did you come up with that? And how did you just remember it just like that?" she asked. I had said it enough times in gigs, and considering it was all about how much I hated being single, I thought it was the most logical and appropriate thing to do.

A few days later, Juliet rang me to tell me Channel 4, and her TV company had seen my video profile and had picked me to appear in the documentary. I was really chuffed considering I knew so many women had gone for the first audition. I wondered if it was because I did stand-up comedy that swayed the decision, but in fact, Juliet simply told me she just found me intriguing.

Channel 4 named the documentary '*Why Am I Still Single?*' and it was all part of a selection of shows Channel 4 put on called 'Dating Season'. I went for the audition knowing what they were after someone who 'should' be married by a certain age, according to society, but life just wasn't like that anymore. When I was chosen to be the main feature for the programme, I thought it was just fun and games, getting my face on TV, promoting my comedy, and something I could look back on and have a giggle. It turned out it was actually quite emotionally draining and brutal. One of the days filming, the crew sent me to a wedding dress shop to try on some dresses, only to remind me that I was 30-year-old single girl miles away in life to even be thinking about which veil I would want to buy for the big day. As I looked at myself in the mirror with the camera crew and Juliet standing around me, I suddenly felt really stupid and I wished I had never taken part. A whole of week of filming included really getting to know who I really was and what I was possibly doing wrong in life. It was like a crash course in therapy. By the end of my journey after what felt like a solid month of filming, being told WHY I was still single was still to come. All my bad qualities highlighted for viewers' entertainment to critic and tweet their opinions on who I was. What made the experience even more gruelling was that David was asked to be interviewed for the show. Knowing he was going to be asked about me and why we weren't back together. I was incredibly shocked he agreed to take part in the first place. While he was filmed, I was placed in a hotel room unable to be in contact with the outside world, that for me was the hardest part.

Watching the show air right in front of me, I sat with my housemates and found watching the show a lot easier than I thought. As I sat with my laptop open on my lap, literally hundreds of tweets and hashtags came flooding in on Twitter, I was utterly terrified about how I would be perceived but what I received on social media was extremely positive. Woman all over the country were relating to my situation, and it was the experience of participating that made me look at myself and grow as a person. I messaged David if he was watching but he point-blank refused to see it. But I was grateful that he took part. The following couple of weeks leading up to Edinburgh, I was being bombarded with messages, questions and people approaching me on the street. I enjoyed every moment, and I learnt so much about myself and was becoming much more self-aware.

Two nights before I was heading off to Scotland, David had invited me to his annual summer garden party and I was torn about going. David has finally watched the documentary and wasn't happy about his perception on the show. But of course, we always seemed to get drawn back towards each other and David knew I was going away for a month, so we didn't need much convincing to spend time together again.

Whilst having some food and drink in the garden, I was talking to some of David's friends about the show, when two girls next door, coincidently watching the show on repeat there and then, at that exact moment heard me in the garden and recognised my voice.

"Hey, Naomi, are you still single?" A shout came from over the garden fence, which stopped everyone dead in their tracks.

"I recognised your voice, Naomi. Tell us, are you still single?" the other girl excitedly shouted while she peered over the fence.

"I'm not sure, ask David," I replied back, looking at David for a grain of hope. He didn't answer. David did, however, ask me later that night if I was dating anyone. I could only smile knowing he was bothered. Jamie had pretty much fizzled out of the picture too by this point so it was great to spend time with David before going away to Edinburgh for a month.

Edinburgh festival 2013 was incredible. '*Why am I still single?*' was also aired in Scotland, so people everywhere seemed to know who I was, which helped me fill my 100-seater venue. I had a little fan base of 14-year-old boys and girls, that even though my show was rated 18, groups of teenagers came to see my show days in a row. Being asked for a photo or an autograph just seemed ridiculous to me, but I just enjoyed every moment while it lasted and happily had photos with who ever asked. I was starting to think I could get used to this kind of attention.

A few days into my show, *The Sun* newspaper came to interview me and do a photo shoot for a double-page interview with fully dressed photos of me—I had to ask, it was *The Sun* after all. I jumped at the chance at more exposure but what a mistake that was. Journalists who could magically craft a conversation into something it isn't. A beautifully warped skill of turning things around, twisting things, changing stories and creating quotes that didn't exist, up from nothing. According to *The Sun*, I started stand-up comedy to find love, and when I couldn't find it, decided to become a lesbian, whilst simultaneously wanting to hook up with Kevin Bridges. I knew then to never let *The Sun* interview me again.

From day one up in Edinburgh, the atmosphere led me to do one main thing. Drink—a lot. I met an established comic called Paul Pirie, who I spent most of the month with. Him being Scottish, drinking was normal to him. When I woke up the following morning, after my first heavy night out, my stomach was eating up my insides and my head was pounding harder that I hadn't experienced since my university days. In my defence, I had spent the night trying to keep up with a Scottish comedian no less. Through my years of nights out and vile hangovers, I had picked up some very unusual tips for curing a hangover. From sleeping on bags of ice to eating pickled herring. But after 27 consecutive days of drinking non-stop at the Edinburgh Festival with Paul, my cure turned out to be too just to carry on drinking. I woke up to a vodka lemonade with a fresh slice of lime, an important segment that contributed to one of my five a day. For brunch, we would down a shot of Sambuca, carry on drinking after our show and to top off the night, we drank pints of cider, colourful cocktails and more shots which seemed like the perfect solution. Until, of course, I knew I would eventually have to stop drinking once I was back in London. And once I returned, the hangover hit me like a ton of bricks, and I was in bed for a week, recovering.

My month up in Edinburgh was one of the best times doing stand-up comedy. I was in my own bubble, around people who were open minded, creative and expressive. I didn't want it to end. I loved Edinburgh, and I loved performing. I received three reviews for my first solo show. It was quite clear when I received them, that I was either loved or hated.

Five Star Review

You may know Naomi Hefter from, 'Why Am I Still Single', but that's not all you should know her from. 'Chaos and Order – A True Story' is a riveting, bawdy, and hilarious hour of brilliance, from someone who is absolutely headed for a bright future in this industry. If you want to see classy and wonderful comedy at the Fringe, this is what you should be seeing—5/5 Stars.

Four Star Review

Naomi Hefter returns to the Fringe for another year, this time taking on her first solo show. 'Chaos and Order' perfectly demonstrates Hefter's trademark honesty—she really doesn't hold anything back. She says exactly what she's thinking, and the majority of the time this is a definite strength. Undoubtedly, a natural comic, all that really lets her down is her lack of patience with the audience—she seems frustrated when things don't go as they ought to. That said there really is nothing else to fault with her performance. Her anecdotes are hilarious, all the more so because of her claim that every story is true. It's not a comfortable comedy (there are awkward moments galore) but that isn't to say it's not funny or enjoyable.

One Star Review

Are you the sort of person who'd like to guess at what age a woman lost her virginity in the hope of winning a 'masturbation wipe'? Then Naomi Hefter's show is the one for you. Graphic filth defines these 50 minutes; that and anecdotes of her appalling behaviour. It's advertised as an 18+ show, but the parents who thought it might be OK for their 13-year-old had to leave in embarrassment as a section about eating cum gave way to her revealing she talked about masturbation on a first date. Thank God they didn't stick around to hear this strange stand-up discuss YouPorn and the size of a fellow comedian's dick, then apologise: 'There's no punch line to that.' And she wonders why she's single…

That last line felt like a kick in the teeth, I wouldn't have minded a reviewer not enjoying my show, but reading how personal he got really threw me. I was told that my one-star reviewer was from a man who was known for disliking female comics, but I couldn't help but take the last line as a personal attack. I felt that he used my material about being single and what made me vulnerable to personally hurt me. And it had worked. I literally felt jab in my stomach and was left infuriated that this stranger had made out I had fluffed my lines when I told the audience I 'didn't have a punch line'. Not having a punch line WAS the joke. I couldn't help but wonder how the man who resembled Mr Burns from the Simpsons even got to review stand-up comedy if he didn't get an obvious joke.

Two nights later, I was invited to the balcony of the Gilded Balloon, where all the very established and famous comedians would drink until the early hours. It was a cool place to be with a beautiful view looking over the city and fancy cocktails to try. And right there, as I carried my drink to the balcony, stood the man who gave me the review. So, I approached him, looked him in the eyes and asked why his review got so personal. I was left shell-shocked when someone so harsh, so opinionated and so unnecessarily spiteful, happened to be the shyest, most awkward man I had ever met. He couldn't even look at me let alone answer my question. He just stood there, meek and pathetic. Was this really the person I had been stressing over for the last 48 hours?

On the last day of the festival, I was one of the last to leave. I couldn't help but have one last stroll around the city, seeing all the posters half hanging off the boards and trodden-on flyers all over the cobbled streets, I felt I had to write some thoughts down there and then.

Diary Extract – August 26, 2013

I stroll down Cowgate in Edinburgh and as I watch the posters get torn down from the many venues, a moment of melancholy flutters around me. Most comics have left the Fringe to go back home and collapse with exhaustion, but I decide to have one last day here alone, to evaluate my experience and think about my somewhat dramatic life. Twenty-seven days have passed, but in the alcoholic bubble of the Edinburgh festival, it feels like I've been here for over a year. People from London have become hazy faces in my mind, feeling planets away. But as I realise this crazy time has to come to an end, I look forward to seeing the familiar faces again. My solo show was called Chaos and Order, and those poignant words have summed up this festival perfectly. With gossip, scandals, rumours, affairs, antics and adventures, all running parallel with the daily routine of the alarm being set every morning, and a show to perform at the same time every day. Within the first week, I'd received a 4-star review with press interest, validation for my work and a few phone numbers thrown into my donation bucket. I felt like Spider-man, only without the ASBO. But I soon came tumbling back down to the cobbled streets with a 1-star review, which hit me hard. But then I felt a little better when I realised that even the best comics get good and bad reviews, and it was written by a spineless little weasel that all along just wanted to be a comic himself.

I'm ashamed to admit, in my four filthy weeks of Chaos and Order, I consumed 42 burgers, 22 pot noodles and 12 pizzas... As well as the 72 units of Captain Morgan Spiced Rum and endless cocktails which caused me to throw up a neon-yellow substance. It was OK to give my broken body a break and live off broccoli juice for the next three weeks back at home. Home... there's no place like home, right? I feel a mixture of apprehension and wonder when I think of what's to come in London. Jobs to find, gigs to book, jokes to write, things to do, people to see, books to read, comics to watch, networking, emailing, filming, sleeping... the list is endless. I do worry that as soon as I step back into my bedroom later tonight, back in the big smoke, I'll be wondering if this experience has been nothing but a lucid dream. A vivid photograph in my mind, filled with a mixture of all the emotions we all felt together. But then I'll be reminded of all the wonderful memories from looking all the drunken funny photos on Facebook. So, until next year, goodbye Edinburgh Festival.

October 11th I was lying in bed with my phone switched off, I didn't want to be disturbed by anyone. I wasn't feeling too well, and it was a refreshing change not to have people around or social media on to disturb me. But I felt the sudden urge to turn my phone on, thinking David was going to contact me. I hadn't seen him since his garden party in July and he was away in Las Vegas for a wedding. When I turned my phone on, within ten minutes, my phone rang. It was David drunk, walking alone in Vegas going back to his hotel room. It made me smile to hear his voice, and I remember feeling a sense of knowing he would contact me and we were going to get back together soon. I was no psychic and I was no fortuneteller either. I just went with my gut. He rang to tell me I was on his mind, and he hoped I was OK and asked to meet up with him once he had returned. The connection between us wasn't going anywhere.

When David had come back to London, we met up at a coffee shop on Church Street. I told him about my Edinburgh adventures, and he showed me the photos of his adventures around the Grand Canyon and the crazy places and foods he had tried. He told me about the amazing clubs in Vegas and how much I would love it there. It was good to see him in front of me in a calm and neutral place. And for the first time in a long time, neither of us asked each other about other potential dates or shenanigans that may or may not have occurred, we were just happy to see each other.

Just when David had returned, one of my flatmates was leaving London for six months to go traveling around India. She found a girl on Gumtree who was looking for temporary living so was going to stay and pay the share of the rent until our housemate came back. I and the third housemate, Alexa, weren't very happy as we hadn't had the chance to meet this new girl. After all, it would be us living with her. So, when I came home one evening to find this new girl not only had moved in, but she had brought a friend to move in with her as well, who would be kipping on the floor, I instantly had a feeling that this setup was not going to go well. The flat was small enough as it was, so to have four people living there, mornings were a nightmare. Mad rushes to the bathroom, not enough room in the tiny kitchen for three, let alone four and the sheer awkwardness of this random person hanging around. Within a few short weeks, Alexa and I asked these two girls to pay more towards the bills, this was only fair, there were two in one bedroom after all. They seemed to take our request quite badly and was suddenly started to make things very difficult for us. Leaving the front door wide open, playing music loudly and eating our food, things were getting out of hand.

One unexpectedly quiet night, while Alexa and I were sitting watching EastEnders together, we noticed there had been less movement and sound coming from the third bedroom in the last 24 hours. The giggling teenage girl that was inside every woman came out of me and Alexa as we dared each other to go and open the girl's bedroom door to see what we could find. After 30 minutes of egging each other on and holding our noses to hold in the sniggering, we both eventually opened her door to discover a completely empty bare room. Everything was gone, including the two girls.

With the two girls doing a runner, no rent had been paid, and no keys had been left. Alexa and I were left to cover her share of the rent for the next three months, and we were panicking whether to change the locks or not. But me being me, I wasn't going to stand for it. All we knew about this girl was her full name, she was originally from Liverpool and that she worked for Sainsbury's. The next day, back at a three-day temp job in the city, I had the internet and a phone, and the time to do some research.

Our little friend, who had scarpered, had a very strong Liverpudlian accent. So, putting on my dreadful impersonation of the Scouse accent, I rang up Sainsbury's head office, and pretended to be her sister who wanted to go in and surprise her at work.

"Please, can you tell me which branch Sophie Turner works at please?" I said, in my dreadful attempt of the strong distinctive Northern tone, accidently spitting on the computer screen as I spoke. Lo and behold, head office told me which branch Sophie worked, and right there and then I rang up the correct shop in London and asked for the manager.

"Hello there, are you the boss of Sophie Turner?" I asked in my own accent, feeling my heart pound a little faster.

"Yes, I am, can I help at all?" said the voice of a polite young man.

"Yes, you can help me, you can tell your employee Sophie Turner that this is Naomi Hefter, and if she doesn't pay the month's rent and bring back our door keys, I will personally turn up to your place of work and make such a scene in front of you and her, she would wish she worked at Tesco!"

The following day, Sophie paid the rent and dropped off the keys, leaving them with the estate agent on our road.

I had been offered a small writing job to review nightclubs for a new online music magazine. It was very low money, but they got me VIP entry, and covered my drinks and taxi's home. One of the clubs I was asked to review was a new nightclub in the O2. It was two weeks before Halloween, and I took a girl I had met through one of my many temp jobs. We had a great night with free drinks and me taking mental notes of the new club which had a giant metal bridge that crossed through the entire giant main dance room. Whilst there, I met a guy called Tom. He approached me by asking me to take a photo of him and his friends, and with some mild flirting, he asked for my number. A week later, he invited me to a Halloween party. On paper, it was the perfect first date, cocktails, laughter, followed by great food and a party to attend. But I always listen to my gut instincts, and I knew something wasn't right. I couldn't put my finger on it, but I knew something just wasn't falling into place with me. After a few more cocktails, and a kiss here and there, there was a sudden interruption of my date being punched in the face by a girl. The snake had a girlfriend. He had told me over dinner he had been single for six months. After the huge display of tears and shouting from this girl, and a slightly swollen eye on my date, he looked incredibly embarrassed as he tried to worm his way out of being caught. I happily left my date and walked out with his girlfriend, who luckily believed me when I told her I thought he was single.

The following morning, I woke up with the most harrowing pain I had ever felt. Waking up to see the right side of my face so ballooned and swollen, I found it disturbing as I looked at myself in the mirror and hardly recognised myself. But as the pain consumed me, I didn't care what I looked like, and I booked an emergency doctor's appointment there and then. I was obviously scared what and why this had happened.

I saw the doctor within an hour just before I had an interview for a temp job in the West End. The doctor told me to immediately go to the Ear, Nose and Throat hospital at Kings Cross. I attended my interview first, apologising for looking like the Elephant man. It was a complete waste of time as the two ladies looked at me like I was some sort of alien who had stuffed the inside of her face with toilet paper. Not only was I struggled to speak, I also failed to sound super enthusiastic when they asked me why I wanted to be a receptionist for an oil and gas company. On my way home, I was in so much pain I contemplated just to go to bed and get some sleep. But as the hospital I was referred to was on my way home, I went in and saw a nurse. After a tube and a camera had been inserted up my nose and down the back of my throat, I was sent a taxi, and was told to immediately go to the general hospital in Euston as they could see my throat narrowing from an infected they suspected I had and was spreading, As I painfully headed to the next hospital, I got there and sat in the waiting room, eyes closed from the pain, feeling nauseous and weak. As I listened to a security guard throw out a drunken Polish man, I was really quite scared what was going to happen to me. It was not what I had in mind for that chilly Monday in November when I should have had was a great interview. I looked at my reflection in my compact mirror, the right side of my face looked as though someone had filled it with a pair of testicles. I was in the most severe pain I had ever experienced in my life. I was told that I had somehow contracted an infection in the back of my throat and fluid around my jaw had become so badly infected, it had devolved into sepsis and was rapidly spreading. Unsure if it was from a tooth or not, the doctor calmly told me that the poison was slowly moving around my face and neck and was eventually going to close my windpipe. I had to have an emergency operation, removing the tooth just in case that was the cause, but they had to also slice open the back of my throat to drain away the poison. My first thought was to call David. Things had been a bit awkward since the TV show and we hadn't really seen each other since we caught up in the coffee shop earlier that October.

Before I knew it, I was lying in a hospital bed, the night before my first ever operation and David was by my side. As I was still in agony, he helped me undress out of my clothes that I still had on from my interview that morning and put me in a clinical white very un-sexy gown. David also took the piss out of the huge spot that I had on my forehead, and sat and hugged me until I fell asleep.

The next morning, unable to eat for 24 hours and on a drip, I felt cold as my bum stuck out of the backless theatre gown. I was drowsy from the medication I had been given to ease the pain and I was about to be put under general anaesthetic, something I had never experienced before, and I was shitting myself. Before I went in for the operation, I texted David saying, "Just in case I don't wake up, I love you." It sounded a little dramatic, but I was incredibly nervous, signing a declaration form in case I didn't wake up from the anaesthesia. David and I hadn't said that we loved each since we had broken up, but I felt it was important to tell him.

I woke up groggy and pain free with an oxygen mask on my face, and blood in my mouth. It was all over. The tooth has gone, the poison had been drained and all I was left with stitches on inside my mouth. Even though I could walk, it was nice to be wheeled back to my hospital bed for one last night to rest. The next morning, I was woken up from a deep sleep to the sound of a high-pitched Spanish man clapping his hands and shouting 'Wakey wakey, darling' at me. I was not impressed. He plumped my pillows and moved the little TV I had in my room close up to my face as though I had just had eye surgery. I was grateful for his attentiveness, but I was looking forward to being back in my own bed. After a mere 72 hours in hospital, my face was looking less like the elephant man and the horrific pain I had felt had subsided into a mild ache from the stitches.

When I got home, I took some time out to rest and I wanted to use my time in bed wisely, so I decided to watch the box set of *Breaking Bad*. I had heard so many positive things about the series but refused to watch it as it had been hyped up to the extent it put me off. Once I watched the first episode, that was it for me. I finished the entire five series in under a week, and adored every moment of the action and comedy timing that had me gripped in every episode. James Morgan McGill, who played Saul Goodman, started his career in stand-up comedy, and I found his persona hilarious in the series. I went on to watch *Breaking Bad* all over again, not too long after I had watched it the first time.

Just when I had fully recovered and was back to life, I was sitting watching *EastEnders* with my flatmates on a chilly November night, when I received a text from David asking me not to date anyone else anymore. "Does this mean we are official, for real this time?" I replied, feeling butterflies flutter around my stomach.

"Yes," was his quick reply.

And with that, we were back together. There was a new chapter to our relationship, and something had changed in him. He hadn't asked me to not see any one else since we first got together in 2006. I didn't tell my flatmates what had just happened, I just went to bed smiling that night.

"'Tis the season to be jolly, fa la la la laaa la la la laaaa. That'll be 14 quid for the two of ya love, enjoy the ride!" I'm not sure I heard that correctly. I had buckled up my boots and wrapped my neon pink scarf around my neck before heading off to Winter Wonderland in the middle of December. I had to brace myself for terrifying three-minute rides David and I used to go on, but since 2008 the prices had drastically rocketed! I felt excited that I had consciously gotten myself into the Christmas spirit, even though friends were still calling me the Grinch. Every year, I went to the fabulous festive place of Winter Wonderland in Hyde Park to receive my annual fix of German sausage and eggnog. This year was extra special as it was David accompanying me. We hadn't been to Winter Wonderland together since 2008. As we entered the gates, gazing upon the gigantic Christmas trees, a man-sized toy soldier and a giant Father Christmas, I couldn't wait get on the Waltzers.

To end what had been such a whirlwind year in 2013, David and I were finally, officially back together, and I felt elevated. I wasn't sure, but maybe my stint in hospital sent him into frenzy which made him realise what he could have lost.

2014

You're Fired!

January 2, 2014. I just had yet another row with my mother. After spending too many days in each other's company, this was the norm. Only this time, we were in the middle of Starbucks with people listening to us. Like every ridiculous row we had, it ended with her screaming, shouting and making a scene, then walking out dramatically. As I watched her leave, she turned and stuck two fingers up at me.

I was yet again, left feeling frustrated, twisted and bitter with our relationship.

I had 50 minutes of nothing to do before catching my coach back to London where I belonged. I was feeling angry, knotted up inside and so resentful. Suddenly, everything around me turned dark and negative, and thoughts swam into my mind, taking over any rational decision. I repeatedly made the mistake of letting her get under my skin and allowing her to press all my buttons she knew would wind me up and hurt me. It was then I pressed my own self-destruct bottom, and went on a shoplifting spree without calming down and thinking clearly. Like anyone who drank a bottle of wine when they got depressed, or overindulged in foods, or picked up a man or woman from a bar to fill their needs for the night, taking items for free gave the rush and the satisfaction I needed. Nothing more than a quick fix to fulfil me and soften the blow of how I was left feeling in Starbucks.

I first walked right into Marks and Spencer's, and picked up the first expensive box of chocolates I found. I didn't even want them, so once I walked out the back entrance and outside, I gave them to a homeless man. I offered the unopened large

114

box of chocolates to him, and with a surprised expression and a twinkle in his eye, he happily accepted the box.

Never really understanding until I had therapy, that shoplifting only came into my life when I was feeling lost, rejected and isolated. My outbursts of taking things was my own way of dealing with pain and fill an emptiness I was feeling. Moments later, I found myself in exactly the same Boots store all those years later, from when I was caught the first time when I was a teenager. I was again ruthlessly taking anything I felt I could get away with. I was a grown adult doing exactly the same thing I did when I was just thirteen years old. And as always, I was stealing things I didn't even want or need. But at the time, I was too wound up and upset to care. As I walked out of Boots, I was stopped by an undercover security guard dressed in normal clothes, hidden in plain sight. I was asked to go into the security office while they checked the security cameras. There they saw me take fake tan, makeup and a hairbrush. As the items totalled to more than £100, the police were called. The officer who turned up watched the security cameras back and could quite clearly see it was me on tape. I was so scared as I had to get my coach back to London and I didn't know what was going to happen. The police officer agreed I could go as long as I gave him all my details for me to return, and make a statement and receive a possible fine or even a criminal record. I got on the coach and burst into tears, knowing I would be hearing from him again. And I did. He called me literally less than 24 hours later and asked me to come back to Cheltenham to make a statement, and that I would be receiving a caution. His name was PC John Simmons and I wasn't prepared for what was to come when I saw him again.

PC Simmons asked to come in and see him the following Saturday, and I went without telling a soul. I got to the station in Cheltenham and went and sat in the interview room. Feeling nervous, I clutched my bag wondering what was going to happen to me. The next six hours were nothing I had ever anticipated. When he arrived, he began by telling me all the police officers had heard about me and wanted to meet me. They were curious about my stand-up comedy, and had spent the morning with PC Simmons googling and discussing what I had done. Within an hour, John and I found ourselves alone in the interview room, talking for hours and hours about each other's lives. There was nothing sexual about it or weird between us, we were just two people who seemed to click and get along so well. We spoke about his first wife and how he met his second, we talked about the pain I was going through without David in my life and the struggles I had with money. It was just an unfortunate, strange situation we were in considering I was someone who had been arrested and bought in for questioning. It was the elephant in the room that neither of us mentioned but it was also something we couldn't forget I knew I had to have a mug shot taken and a formal warning was going to be placed. If I was ever to get caught shoplifting again any time before my 36th birthday, I would automatically be fined or sent to court. Before I had turned up to the police station that morning, I had bought myself a new black sparkled top from Primark. It was £3 in the sale, and considering it was so detailed and well made, I had to buy it. As I knew I was going to have my mug shot taken, I told myself I should at least look a little glam for the photo, so I asked John before he took the shot if I could change and with roaring laughter, he stepped out of the room to let me put on my mug shot outfit. He came back into the room still chuckling as I stood there in my top that sparkled and shone. He took my photo as I posed like I was being photographed for a fashion magazine. John gave me a nod, we were done. I felt a sense of relief, realising that I had put myself in a seriously bad situation but there were still good people out there who were there to help and be understanding. John's position and his authority left the room that day, and he had clearly broken the rules with all the things we had talked about, but we were just two people who met in strange circumstances who clicked, and talked about life, love and the future.

John offered to drive me to the coach station for me to head back to London. I cheekily asked him if he turn on the sirens with the flashing blue police lights, and he did. As we soared full speed through the streets of Cheltenham with sirens blazing above our heads, we laughed, and I was almost sad to go home. I could have made a friend that day, but he had a job to go back to and I had London calling my name.

Later that year, to my surprise, John posted me a birthday card. He told me that police officers and offendants were not allowed to exchange gifts, foods, tickets for shows, letters or any type of thank you but in the card, it read, "You are a breath of fresh air. Keep your nose clean and you can do whatever you want in life." There was also a lottery ticket inside. I sent him a letter the following day, and thanked him for my card and ticket. I never heard from him again.

With an eventful start to 2014, I was also offered an exciting gig that same month. My first gig at The Glee Club in Birmingham. I was to travel by coach, there and back, and be home in bed by 1 am as I had a two-week temp job I had to get back to in the morning. When I turned up to The Glee, I found myself in the green room with Mark Dolan, Russel Kane and Mark Watson, and I suddenly felt like a little sardine fish in a large river. But my gig went really well, considering the audience was as large as the Comedy Store and I always felt more nervous in venues I had never played in before. But I remember asking myself while I sat back stage, why I couldn't be proud of myself, knowing how far I had come since my first ever gig. I never felt I did a good enough job and continuously felt that I could have done better.

That same week I had my gig at The Glee, I also had a hot date booked in. This was not a first date with the guy in question, it was possibly the 300th date. It was with David. With all the first dates I had been on over the space of almost five years, I was determined for someone to catch my attention long enough to make me move on, but none of them quite lived up to the infamous ex. Going back out with an ex was like trying on different outfits for a Friday night out with the girls, you always ended up wearing the first outfit you tried on.

Spending more and more time with David was interesting, because even though I knew this time was different than the other times before, I was still very wary, insecure and feeling doubtful of what was going to happen. I didn't want to get hurt again but I loved every moment we had together.

By February, Pancake Day had come, and David came over to my place to do some flipping with me. My pancakes always turned out burnt or thick, soggy and undercooked. David, being the great cook he always had been, made me six perfectly thin pancakes with a crispy edge drenched in golden syrup which I ate in under 10 minutes. I felt really good that we were officially back together, and things were going well, but I was conscious that I was moving at a snail's pace just to protect my heart. Deep down, I knew this was it and all I wanted was for it to work out this time.

I had reached a time in my life where even though I hadn't told anyone I was taking Citalopram and I knew I had some serious underlining issues which I knew I had to face sooner or later. Understanding that I needed CBT was vital now David and I were back together, and I was determined for us not to go down the same road again and make all the stupid mistakes I had made before. More importantly, I knew I needed to have the therapy for myself as I didn't want to be on Citalopram forever. I went through the NHS and as I guessed, there was a long waiting list. I was prepared to wait, and I knew once I started the sessions that I was going to be given exercises and tools to train myself out of how I saw myself and the world around me and I was prepared to work at it.

Diary Extract

There are moments in life when I feel so nostalgic and miss being the innocent child that I once was. With the ignorance of never realising anything was wrong and I thought life was going to be easy peasy. Saturday afternoons in the mid-1990s was all about meeting up with friends in town, going to the cinema and stopping off on the way to get some sickly-sweet sugar-coated Pick 'n Mix and Cherry Panda Pops. Woolworths may have died over the last Year, but I still remembered and missed it because it was part of my early years. Peter Andre's Mysterious Girl single sold for 99p, pencil cases were bought every season, and you could buy a ghetto blaster for £9.99 that would break four months later. I almost forgot in this chaotic world that days when I could buy a £10 phone top-up card that made me and my friends feel like proper grown-ups. Finding myself working in Woolworths when I was fifteen wasn't much fun when I found myself up on the fourth floor in the kid's department. During the Christmas holidays, dressed in a turquoise oversized shirt and a knee-length navy blue skirt that felt like carpet rolled up around me. It's only when you are an adult, and you look back at those moments and realise, even amongst the torment I lived with from Bill, life was, in so many ways simple and dreams felt like only an arm's reach away.

I was back on the temping scene again and my first assignment that year was quite possibly, one of the worst jobs I had ever encountered. I would be working at reception for the NHS on Peckham Road, which was miles away from anywhere. So, to start with, the commute was such a pain in the arse. Three tube changes, then either an over-packed bus for twenty minutes or a long walk in the rain for forty minutes. On my first day, I had chosen the bus, but the traffic was so bad, I got off half way there and walked until I realised there was not one shop in sight to pick up any lunch, and my shoes were soaked from the February rain. Turning up late, I was already in a foul mood and it got worse when I started work. I was told I would be signing people in at a doctor's waiting room, simple enough, but within my first hour, I was asked to sort out a large sack of post. As a receptionist ten times over, I was used to the large quantities of post get dragged in daily, usually by a super enthusiastic happy go lucky mailman. On this particularly rainy miserable morning, miles from civilisation, I was given the unusually large mail sac. As I put my arm in the sack, ready to pull out a handful of letters, I pulled out a leg. A very small leg, may I add. I dropped it like a hot potato from pure shock. And amongst the packaging, there were also arms and feet. It was at that point I prepared myself to find a head in there. Happy to report back that no head was found. I was hoping the next two weeks weren't going to be pure hell. I could make my own lunch to bring in, walk to work for the exercise and get used to the arms and legs in the post. By the time I had finished dealing with the bag of limbs, it was still raining out, and with my body stiff from being folded up inside the tiny two-by-two-foot staff room, the morning had felt like a year. There was no lunch that day, so with nothing but a weak cup of tea from the machine that cost 20p, I just went and sat back down at reception to work the day away. Suddenly, a lady approached me asking, "Please, can you watch my child while I go in for my appointment?" My heart stopped. My mouth dried up and so did my uterus. That was the ultimate ask, considering I wasn't a fan of babies. Plus, I didn't even know how to look after myself, let alone a crying infant. As the lady rushed into her appointment, I was left with who I assumed was her child as he sat on the reception desk and dribbled onto my keyboard. I failed the one-week assignment by not turning up the next day. They never heard from me again. The million-mile journey in the rain, dishing out limbs and holding bendy wet babies was not worth the £9.40ph.

For the first time in a long time, I got a job, which on paper, seemed too good to be true. I would be temping for a media company in Shoreditch. They published magazines and the location was perfect. I could have been perfectly happy there. The people seemed fun, the hours were great, and it was up the road from my house. I had only been there for two weeks when the receptionist returned, so I was a little disappointed as I had started to settle in on the top floor. But instead of leaving, I was asked to move to the second floor as I was offered a job in the sales department. I was to sell advertising space for on flight magazines. I was feeling optimistic to be doing something other than reception work.

Hindsight is a beautiful thing. I thought I hated being a receptionist that was until I tried sales. For years, people had commented I had the ability and personality to sell, sell, sell. These people didn't know me at all! I was confident to talk to people, I was able to sound passionate, but I didn't enjoy talking to people about things I had no interest in, I was not savvy or ruthless enough and I was never motivated by money. The sales environment was a whole new world to me. It was cut throat, it was fast paced, and this sales team was full of arrogant twats. My boss, who had the selling skills of a genius but the manners of a slug, often grabbed his stumpy cock through his pin striped trousers while telling me he could 'do things that no one else could do', or telling me I was a useless, ugly, unfunny person who should give up comedy and stick to sales.

Each morning in the office, the routine started with him throwing rugby balls at my boobs. Yes, we had to play rugby every morning to 'warm up our sales juices'. So, every morning, my breasts or my vagina would be bruised and abused with extreme throws of a rugby ball, before having to sit opposite my sweaty chauvinistic boss.

Sales for me was quite literally draining my soul. I had to make exactly 100 calls a day to companies asking if they wanted to be advertised in the magazine. This wasn't a sales job, it was a call centre job with every person hanging up on me. I was feeling stressed, on edge and incredibly annoyed with myself for putting up with the shit from my boss. Plus, having to read on Facebook that comics were starting to mention Edinburgh Festival and I couldn't go as I simply couldn't afford it that year.

Exactly one month into working in sales, after many episodes of me crying in the toilets, I knew I couldn't stay much longer. I got a phone call from the agency that found me the job in the first place. My sweaty, arrogant, derogatory boss had told the agency I had stripped in front of the office and made advances towards him. I found myself screaming and crying, and raging down the phone, hoping the agency didn't believe such absurd lies. I marched straight to HR where I told them what the agency had said. I was calmed down by a lovely Irish lady, Broner who offered to get my bag as I was adamant to leave there and then. Over the next few days, she emailed me checking up that I was OK. I was just fed up.

Ten days later, I was offered a job in a tall office block near Euston. The job didn't come with uniform instructions, but I was told to dress corporate and look polished. I already knew if this place was corporate, I probably wasn't going to fit in, but I needed the cash, plus, it was only a two-month contract. Turning up on my first day wearing a smart navy-blue suit, my hair tied up and my makeup perfectly applied, I didn't expect to be asked to go out shopping on my first day.

I walked into the reception area where I was told that my navy-blue suit was inappropriate and that I must go out and buy a black suit immediately. I was wearing a navy-blue suit, not a neon-pink body stocking. I remember thinking that unless I went out and stole a damn suit, which wasn't a good idea, I wouldn't be able to buy one as I simply didn't have the money. So, they had a choice; fire me on the spot or ring the agency to sort a suit out for me. The agency was called, and I was told they could get a jacket for me to borrow as soon as possible.

Fifteen minutes later, I was sitting at the desk wearing a borrowed black blazer, in a Size 20. Looking and feeling like a tosser, I suggested my size 8 navy blazer might look a little better. No, the black blazer was insisted. It was at that moment, I took off the borrowed blazer that swamped me, and walked out.

There was a silver lining. David and I had made the decision to do a road trip down the East Coast of America in September, so I had plenty of time to save. Every year in June, I put on an annual car boot sale in Dalston where I sold all my old and unwanted belongings, and managed to make a fair amount of money which helped pay towards the trip, I was sent a tax rebate. I had worked for that many temp jobs, I had accumulated tax, so I was sent a cheque for £1,200. Happy days.

A week or so later, I was offered to an on-going temp with no interview where they needed a receptionist at a very old-fashioned stuffy investment company near Trafalgar Square. It was only a few weeks until David and I would be flying to New York so as much as the corporate world was clearly not right for me, I took the job and told myself it wasn't forever. I almost found it amusing that these job agencies who claimed they knew me so well, kept placing me in these cooperate companies.

I was working alongside four other women. All late 40s and above. I was worried they wouldn't make me feel welcome, but they were all really lovey. They had all been there for years and had been happy working there. Until there was a big change, a new boss. They couldn't stand that much they named her The Hitler Child. I hadn't met her yet but as I knew we were the same age, it made me feel better to think that we might be on the same wavelength

Half an hour into my first day, in the sweltering summer heat, I was dressed head to toe in dated polyester I had been given me to wear. A dark-blue knee-length skirt that was exactly like one that I wore when I worked at Woolworths; like a piece of carpet rolled up around me. Thick, shiny, skin-coloured tights that didn't match the rest of my skin, a heavy looking blazar an air hostess might have worn in 1989 that had to be done up, a cheap ill-fitted shirt and a turquoise, fake silk scarf to tie around my neck. We weren't allowed water at the desk even in the heat. No Internet. No phone. Hair up in a bun. Two-inch heels. Shirt tucked in. Name badge on. No earrings. No nail varnish. No lipstick. No fucking life. It was horrific. I was there just to get the job done, sit politely throughout the day and get paid, But the boss, who despite being the same age as me, acted like a 50-year-old as she spotted the small cluster of stars that were my tattoos on the side of my feet, and my Taurus tattoo and stars on my wrists. Although they were tucked away under the desk for no one to see, she stood right behind me, placing her hands on my shoulders, got me up and walked me to Boots to show me which plasters to buy to cover my tattoos, like a patronising head mistress. Covering them all with plasters made me look like I was trying to hide some sort of rabid foot disease, and around my wrists I suddenly looked I had recently slit them open. I looked ridiculous

Two weeks into the job, the heat had reached the dizzy heights of 33 degrees and I took my jacket off at the desk. My hair was fuzzy around the edges from the humidity, and the plasters had peeled off around my wrists. The Hitler Child told me to go and buy new plasters, and put my jacket on. With her talking down to me like I was an infant, I had enough. It was then I told her what I had thought of her and how she spoke to the four of us on the front desk. The next thing I knew, I was being escorted off the premises. I managed to tell her in time what her nickname was too, pretended it was me who had made up the name so to not get the other ladies in trouble. I didn't look back as I walked away from the building.

Being fired once again was beginning to look like a bad habit that I couldn't shake off. Making the same mistakes repeatedly was getting to me. But I could not conform to office politics so a huge part of me also didn't give a shit because I knew I would never be happy staying in an environment like that anyway.

It was only a matter of days before David and I were ready for our trip where I experienced my shortest job in history. I had been offered a three-week temp role in Mayfair when I was to return from America. I would be a PA to a very prestigious lady. The night before my first day, the agency had forwarded me an email she wanted to pass to me. It read: "Dress for the job that you want, not for the job that you have." I knew I wouldn't last a week with the woman, so I turned up dressed exactly for the job that I wanted. I arrived dressed up as a clown. As the boss took one look at my pillar-box red wig and matching nose, I was fired on the spot.

I had never been more excited about our American trip that was just around the corner. The sun was scorching in the city of London and at the exact same time, the best performance festival in the world was taking place and I wasn't there. Edinburgh Festival. That bittersweet nostalgic notion bubbled up and swamped me while I felt a little sick with jealousy. I knew I wasn't going to miss the hangovers, I knew I would save myself a lot of cash and I knew I wouldn't be gaining half a stone in weight from all the junk I would consume. But maybe I wanted all of that. I wanted to wake up with filthy shoes, spilt red wine and crusty mascara from a party I would have gatecrashed. I even wanted to gain that extra half a stone at the end of the festival, to show how much fun I'd had. The memories and the attachments from the last three years in Edinburgh were still ripe in my mind. To not be part of it in 2014 made me a solemn feeling flutter in the pit of my stomach. The previews, the posters, the flyers, the reviews, the parties, the free shows, the paid shows, the dramas and romance, the fights, the late nights, the early mornings, the gossip, the hangovers, the sunsets, the sunrises, the mess, the preps, the props, the junk food, the drinks, the discounts, the new friends, the old friends, the flings, the relationships, the enemies, the competitions, and the fabulous memories that I'll be missing that year.

I had booked some gigs to do in New York before driving down to Orlando Florida and stopping off at lots of places in between. We also had plans to meet up with Povs in New York, as she was getting a flight from Chicago to stay with us there. It was going to be one of those trips I would never forget.

New York to Washington, to Virginia, to North Carolina, to Savannah, to Jacksonville, to Daytona Beach, to Orlando. It was incredible how within only a few miles between two parts of America, how different they could be. We had experienced so many different cultures, life styles, foods and people. But one of our nights was stood to a halt. An unbelievably huge crazy storm that had very quickly swept across the beach. The rain threw drops the size of fifty pence pieces which didn't stop. The water got higher and higher against the door of our little motel room where we stayed in with a box of Lucky Charms and some Bud Lime-A-Ritas. We had no choice but to flick though the 44 channels our TV offered. We found that the programs were either people selling food products, true crime documentaries or Spanish soap operas. We ended up watching a crime documentary called *Forensic Files* which was really interesting. It showed us how every murder would always leave the tiniest bit of evidence or DNA for forensic experts to crack the case. The channel played one series back-to-back, so after twelve episodes about murder, homicide, arson, manslaughter and bizarre affairs, we found ourselves getting really into it, almost a bit TOO much. I was almost disappointed when we woke the next morning, to find the storm had passed and left behind a clear blue sky, we wanted to watch more Forensic Files!

When we got back to London, we managed to find every single episode of *Forensic Files* on YouTube. Sixteen whole series with up to thirty episodes in each to watch! I questioned if my excitement was normal and tried to keep it under control without looking a little odd. But we both had an interest in crime, and we enjoyed guessing who we thought the killer was in each twenty-minute episode.

A week back in the real world, the perfect timing came along when I was offered a short-term job for a very famous charity. A charity that promotes being healthy, The British Heart Foundation in Camden. I turned up on my first day, this time not doing reception. Instead, I was to take calls from people who wanted tips and advice on healthy eating, and exercise. However, when I turned up on my first day, I noticed there were plates of biscuits and trays of donuts laying around for people to eat. I couldn't get my head around a charity that promoted a healthy heart had so many bad foods behind the computer screens. "Oh, there is only 3.6g of saturated fat in this donut, that's alright!" one lady said as she gorged on a bright pink sugary donut.

I've often heard people say that to be a 'good' comedian, you need to be highly intellectual, be especially good at the English language and know a lot about the world and current affairs. I wouldn't put myself in the 'intellectual' box considering I knew nothing about a lot of topics that some comics talked about, especially when it came to the future of politics, the history of politics and most of all, today's politics. But when I meet someone, a comic or not, I never tried to sound or be any more intelligent than I was, I felt people would see straight through the bullshit. So, when I worked with people in my day jobs with people who tried to sound more intellectual, not only see right through it, but I also wanted to turn the other way and run for being them being so pretentious. During my time at The British Heart Foundation, I got seated next to a lad with the hairstyle of what looked like, a giant walnut whip sat on top of his head. After a few mere hours, I couldn't help but notice his use of the English language, and how he was trying his best to sound more intelligent than he actually was. It started with the words 'figuratively speaking' and 'fundamentally', a fair few times to the boss. But then the word 'essentially' started to pop up, not just to the boss, but to everyone, far too often. I started to feel myself getting agitated when he started using 'essentially speaking', at the beginning of every single sentence. I started to grind my teeth when he slipped in 'essentially speaking', when it wasn't necessary. I then wanted to knock his walnut whip head off when he added 'essentially', when it didn't even make any sense. "You can ring back essentially anytime, Mrs Thomas." By day five of having the word 'essentially' burned into my brain, I decided I could either be sent down for 20 years for a very messy murder, or I could try and enjoy listening to the funny strung-together sentences that left this mouth. So, I made the decision to count how many times he said 'essentially' in one hour. Between 1 pm and 2 pm, it had reached TWENTY-TWO essentials. The twitching of my face at that point was a mixture of bemusement and pain.

I was still working for the charity six weeks later, and I quickly fell into a dangerous robotic routine. I got into work at

8:55 am, I would eat an egg roll from Pret and drink a can of Red Bull. I would check emails before deleting them. I would check the Daily Mail and then make a cup of weak tea. I would make another cup of watery weak tea before opening the post. I would hand out the post, attempt to have a poo, fail and then go to lunch. Once I was back from lunch, I would check the Daily Mail website again to see how many green arrows I got from my comment under each story. I would answer the phone and do the job I was paid to do for a bit before having a good cry. I would frank the post, then at 5:30 pm on the dot, I would run out the office to a gig to make a room full of strangers laugh.

I wrote a poem to help me deal with the rut and the reality that was my life.

Inspired

Working 9–5, what a way to make a living! I hate those words Dolly sings,
working in an office, I can't put into words the misery it brings.

Boring old small talk 'nice evening, nice weekend, nice lunch?'
Listening to the office geek, ya know, the IT guy u wanna punch.

Checking the Daily Mail website 72 times a day,
staring at the computer screen hoping an alien can take me away.

I go to the toilets to masturbate, 36% of you do too!
While biscuits are passed around the office and the office fatty justify herself a few.

Making endless cups of tea, just to pass the time away,
ordering some extra stationary, I think I'll nick a stapler today.

My boss is a right cock, the post guy's a perv,
the office gossip's a cunt, she'll get what she deserves.

We only work in the office to pay off our bills and rent,
I think I'll give up office work, well, at least for next year's
Lent.

So, for now, I'll carry on as an office temp, with my soul
cracked in half,
and the day I'm no longer in the office, I can look back and
laugh.

I always had a belief that no matter what someone wished to become in life, anything that involved hard work and being 'out there', inevitably at some point in the journey towards success, self-doubt and negative thoughts would always somehow creep in. Are you good enough? What about the competition? Will I ever make it? Do I deserve this? Am I too different? Will people get me? Am I letting myself be too vulnerable with my honesty? These questions entered my head and I had found, with stand-up comedy, there were so many highs and lows. Wanting to be liked, working hard to be accepted and understood, trying to get your voice heard. Being rejected, heckled, criticised, you name it, I saw it so often when a comic, new or established, would die on their arse on stage, and all of their new material would flop and fail and some audience members relished on that. So many people unfortunately wanted the act to crash and burn. I saw it time and time again, and more often than not, those were the people who were too afraid to try stand-up comedy themselves. It was those empty insecure people who put people down to make themselves feel better and worked to grind down the sparkle someone had to feed their own insecurities.

But there were the highs too. From time to time, I would find a Facebook message or a Tweet from an audience member who saw my set and loved my work, or a new comic on the circuit who contacted me, asking for advice because they had heard good things about me. These were the things that kept me going. Those audience members who went to watch comedy for the simple fact they wanted to laugh. People who weren't judging, or afraid of comedians who might be a little bit different.

It was also good to see more females on the circuit, and even better that more off the wall and controversial comedy from men and women was being bought back into sets. Comedy had become safe and too politically correct, and it needed to move away from that. Comedy, after all, like poetry and song writing, was freedom of speech, being able to express opinions, thoughts and feelings. Personally, I was focused on writing a new hour of material in preparation for a show the following year. I had spent days staring at blank sheets of paper, trying to think and create new fresh material. But then it dawned on me, I didn't need to worry too much, I was ready to perform the style of comedy I held huge love for; Physical comedy.

As I started to put together my show, I was interviewing for summer jobs. I had been to an interview in Dalston for another reception job that was paying peanuts. I had already embarrassed myself in the interview when I was asked if I knew anything about the company and the man who started up the business. The only thing I knew was that the man designed clothes and made supermodels wear them on a catwalk.

"Well, I know he designs very expensive high fashion clothes, which if you ask me are too overpriced but hey, I'm a Primark gal," I said, to sound light-hearted. However, the man interviewing me leaned forward slowly and calmly said, "I think my brother's hard work has paid off and is right to sell them at those prices."

I left the interview feeling foolish as I had just insulted the brother of JW Anderson himself. As I walked home through Dalston high street in the blazing hot sun, negative thoughts were swamping my brain, assuming my stupid sense of honest humour had lost me the job. I was thirty-one and still temping. Thirty-one and nowhere near anywhere I wanted to be in life. Thirty-one and looking dumb in an interview. It was only then I had the original physical comedy moment: I slipped over on a banana peel, right onto my back. The ultimate famous clown action. It hurt like hell but that old school comedy inspired me to think about what physical comedy I was going to add into my second solo show…

CVs and interviews—the two things that couldn't survive without the other. With the amount of jobs that jumped around the three sheets of paper I called my CV, I knew I came across better in the interview situation, apart from when I told the truth or tried to crack jokes. My CV was far too honest, and I was repeatedly told by job agents to remove doing stand-up comedy from my hobbies and interests' section, as if stand-up comedy was something I needed to hide. According to some companies, mentioning my love of performing would only cause concern for my commitment for the role. Surely, working two jobs would have highlighted that I was a committed person? I just happened to walk out of a lot of jobs I couldn't stand. I had lost count how many times I had to explain to interviewers that stand-up comedy was a nighttime activity, like any other hobby after work. One of the most frustrating questions I was asked during interviews when stand-up comedy was brought up, "How do you get up every day for work with a hangover?" The ignorant assumption that not only I drank after every gig, but that I gigged every night too! If only!

If it were up to me, I would write up and send a CV that would say the truth. No fluff, no sugar-coating just the information we really want to give;

Curriculum Vitae

Objective

My dream job would be a writer/author but right now, to get a simple job with not too much responsibility would be good so I can write a book. I have no intention of being a receptionist for long but I have plenty of experience, for I'm devilishly charming. I won't steal stationery either, I already have plenty of my own.

Skills

Multi-tasking—looking like I'm listening and nodding while the office gossip talks rubbish to me.
Making a cup of tea under 10 seconds.
Deleting unwanted emails and getting rid of annoying cold callers.

Writing poems.
Getting toothpaste off any item of clothing.

Employment History

Around 200 jobs in five years.

Hobbies and Interests

I am an up-and-coming stand-up comedian who enjoys going to the theatre, but I don't get paid enough to see as much as I would like.
I also love anything to do with murderers, true crime and why people commit such horrific murders. Hope this doesn't put you off.

Once my foot was in the door to get the interview, it was the same thing all over again but in person. I was always asked the same stupid interview questions and I always wanted to answer the obvious answers that everyone really knows are true.

Interview Questions

Tell me a bit about yourself

I'm a creative, genuine person who loves to entertain. I also have an addiction to shoplifting and I really hate being single.

Why do you want the job?

Because I need the money, obviously.

Where do you see yourself in 5 years?

I hate being asked this question, because nothing in life goes to plan, does it. But if you want an honest answer, I want to be inspiring people with my stories and helping people realise that anything in life is possible. I can't see myself doing reception much longer, I'd like to have written a book and if it was to be made into a movie, that would be the cherry on the cake. I like to think big. That's where I see myself in five years, but I need to be realistic, hence why I'm here.

What are your strengths?

My time management skills are good and I'm very organised. My wardrobe is lined up in colour coordination and my DVDs are in genre.

What are your weaknesses?

I occasionally cry at work because I hate all the shit jobs I get. I also have a fibroid called Gary from consuming too much processed red meat and Red Bull but he doesn't affect my work.

Do you have any questions for us?

I do. If you could wake up tomorrow and automatically know how to speak every language in the world, speak to animals or know how to play every musical instrument, which would you pick and why?

The year was almost over, and it was time for Halloween. I loved getting into the fancy-dress spirit and I had watched YouTube videos on how to paint on the perfect Sugar Skull face with the added electric blue wig with fairy lights piled on top of my head. There were many of us that night, starting out at David's house for a party. Costumes included a Mad Hatter, Freddie Kruger, a crazy doll, a dead wrestler, the Saw puppet, and what I thought was a frog, happened to be a Ninja Turtle.

Fast forward 12 hours and sitting slung over the bathroom sink, I was still wearing the black bralette from the night before. As I desperately tried to scrub off the glitter, glue, paint and shimmer, the semi-permanent eyeliner was not budging. But as I looked at my hung-over face in the mirror, I smiled knowing me and David were back together.

A few days later, ITV producers had somehow got hold of my number and kept ringing to ask me to audition for the 2015 *Britain's Got Talent*. I told them there was more chance of Simon Cowell teaching his dogs to speak English than me taking part. I was simply not interested and knew my material was too risqué for family audiences to watch. But they kept on ringing, urging me to go on as the show were really keen to have more comedians on that year. I was also contacted by an established comedy agent who was putting together a showcase of comedians who wanted to take part on *Britain's Got Talent*. It was then I obliged. The showcase was held at the Hen and Chicken theatre in Islington, and with a theatre full of ITV producers, the agency and a real audience, I could only see it as a good thing. I treated it like any other gig with the added bonus to get my name out there. As much as I wasn't interested in being on *Britain's Got Talent*, I was suddenly very nervous before walking on stage. But the producers loved my set and the agent approached me, offering me a paid gig. But as I predicted, my material with subjects that included Fred West and shoplifting were a little out there for ITV's target audience. Was I prepared to change my style that I had built and crafted for BGT? I wasn't.

Straight after the audition, I landed a role in a new comedy magic show on E4 called *Look into My Eyes*. It was only for a few days, but like most TV work, it was great money and, of course, I felt at home as I played the part of a waitress having to do ridiculous off the cuff things with hidden cameras filming people who had supposedly been hypnotised. Getting my face out there was really helping me get longer stage time in comedy clubs and my name really known on the circuit.

Every December, everyone knew by now I always morphed into the Grinch. For so many years, my feathers were ruffled, knowing that so many people felt the need to put up a front for the festive period. The streets got so busy you couldn't walk a flea, the couples seemed to magically appear, kissing under the rotten mistletoe. Everyone who was usually miserable and rude in London was suddenly oh so jolly!

But my Grinch heart had finally grown a few sizes bigger than it was. Why? Because I had become one of those cheesy couples. And I was very happy about that. Choosing gifts, wrapping them up, writing that sentimental message in a card. These were the moments I loved being back with David.

Christmas that year was exciting too, as we had been invited to spend it with my Uncle Joe and Aunty Tracey in Sweden. Visiting my modest little Hefter family, plus going with David, I was feeling over the moon, and it was a world away from the miserable Christmases I had spent alone. My Uncle Joe, who was my mother's brother, was more like a father to me than my dad or step dad ever was. My Aunty Tracey, who I loved from the day I met her, was perfect for Uncle Joe. They were two people who really did love each other. They were meant to be together and once they were married, they had two children, Joe and Ezme. When it came to the Hefter side of my family, there had always been a tradition where the first son was called Joseph, pronounced Yosef. To make things easier for everyone, my granddad was called Big Joe, my uncle has always been known as Little Joe, and my cousin simply was known as Cousin Joe.

I had always told myself I wanted my Uncle Joe to be the one to walk me down the aisle when I got married. Once his daughter, my cousin Ezme was born, I changed my mind, worried he would want to save that moment for her. But then I remembered that my uncle had been there for me throughout my life, so I reassured myself that if I was to ever ask him, I knew he would be honoured.

Growing up in Cheltenham with Uncle Joe and Aunty Tracey nearby, I had great memories of them. Before they met, my uncle had moved in with my mother and me when I was a child, and for a while it was just the three of us. Listening to Pink Floyd and watching funny films together. When Uncle Joe met Tracey, life became even better for him and I didn't realise it at the time as I was so young, but my uncle was a little lost in life, but with his forever optimism and sense of humour, I could only see that shine from him. As soon as Tracey turned up, I remember them being so happy as they never left each other's side. It really was true love. In the summer of 2002, they let me move to their house just before I went to university. I hadn't spoken to my mother for over three years and I was stuck for a place to live while I worked in a pub. The one housemate I lived with often had random people over to get stoned in the living room which I hated. I had grown up with my mother rolling a joint every morning, so I didn't want to be around that anymore. I worked long double shifts at the pub so wasn't always at the flat, but when I started to notice fleas jumping around the living room, I wanted to leave. The final straw was when they forgot about food in the oven and set the kitchen on fire. I had to get out of there. I was so relieved and grateful that my Uncle Joe and Tracey had been so kind to let me stay during that summer. The only embarrassing memory I wish I could forget was when the neighbours who lived across the road saw me dance naked in front of a full-length mirror. Tracey tactfully told me to draw the curtains from then on.

When the Hefter family moved to Sweden in 2005, I only got to see them every other summer when they came back and had a get together in Cheltenham, always hiring out the same pub in Leckhampton that sold the best cider. So finally visiting my Uncle, Aunty and two cousins in Sweden in 2014, I knew I was long overdue. They were living literally in the middle of a deep forest in Southern Sweden. I had images of deep snow, arctic foxes and Scandinavian supermodels wearing nothing but a Santa hat walking around the woods. I had only been half joking when I messaged Tracey on Facebook, asking if they had running water and electricity. So, when David and I turned up on Christmas Eve to see they had a beautiful home with a toilet rather than a hole in the ground, I was relieved and felt a tad stupid. Christmas day was wonderful. Champagne for breakfast, duck, turkey and chicken for lunch and company I loved. Being with David for the first time on Christmas day since 2008 was really special for me. I loved that my uncle Joe and Tracey held a tradition of playing board games after Christmas lunch. It was proper family time, and I was a little envious I had never grown up with those times around me.

On Boxing Day, we all took a trip to the cinema to watch *The Hobbit*, as Tracey and my cousin Ezme loved the story. This was when the images of a different time I had in my head came to life. Walking in to what looked like a bingo hall, there sat a lad around 18 years old, behind a table covered in a fresh white table cloth with what resembled a tin can to collect the money from bought tickets. No till, no card machine, we were no longer in 2014. We had been zapped back to 1955. I went off to buy some popcorn and a drink. There, at the end of the table, lay 5 bags of popcorn covered in a layer of dust with a carton of orange juice. It was at this point I just smiled at the simple world they lived in and understood why my Uncle had been so much happier living this uncomplicated life in Sweden.

I did suffer from cabin fever after being held in the middle of the forest for five days. I was missing my creature comforts, the big city, English TV and the busy shops. But just being able to relax with nothing to do but watch films, play games and go for walks in the forest with the family. I knew I had to go with the flow and this had always been difficult for me. Tracey had noticed that I was somewhat agitated and that I distant with everyone. The thoughts of the New Year had been on my mind for a few weeks and I felt anxious, unsure and troubled by the prospect of my CBT I was to begin in January. I knew if I had explained to her what was coming up in my life, and how down I was about my job situation, she would have just smiled, given me a hug and tell me everything was going to be OK. I wish that I had opened up, and told Tracey about it all considering she had this way of seeing everything so calmly and clearly with her natural positivity. But I didn't tell her, or Uncle Joe, or even David how I felt. To them, I was nothing more than someone who came across pretty miserable. Inside, I was so happy to be there that Christmas, with David next to me and seeing family I loved, but that familiar feeling was coming back to me. All the positive things, including CBT was entering life, and I was struggling to let them in.

2015

Ecstasy!

Diary Extract – January 9th

Another year—2015, and I can't help but ask myself—HOW is 'Celebrity' Big Brother still going? The word celebrity is used lightly here, considering the last three years have had very few real celebs entering the house. But this year takes the biscuit. Does appearing on Embarrassing bodies or playing the part of the mouse in the 1987 Cinderella pantomime make you a celebrity? As I looked at the line-up, recognising only Patsy Kensit and 'Cheggers' I couldn't help but wonder; was I famous enough to enter the CBB house next year?

I'm not ashamed to admit I used to watch BB and CBB back in the day when it was good. Seeing the likes of Jack Dee, Michael Barrymore, Ulrika Johnson and Julian Clary. REAL celebrities were actually interesting to watch. The same went for the normal Big Brother years ago. With every day people interacting with other normal people and a few eccentric people thrown in made the show so much more fascinating to watch. What I find fascinating, is now, even the 'normal' Big Brother house contestants have minor contacts to the glitzy world of showbiz. It seems both CBB and BB have kind of merged into one melting pot of clones.

So, me, Naomi Hefter, one-time star of Channel 4's documentary, Why Am I Still Single? My one time 7-page modelling spread, current stand-up comedy career and even that speaking part I had on skins! But as my cousins' uncles' dads' dog isn't a singer and I haven't had an affair with a politician, I wasn't going to hold my breath for that CBB offer any time soon.

My cognitive behavioural therapy had finally approached. I was suddenly feeling sick thinking about what I was going to go through. I honestly didn't know what to expect, but all I knew was I had waited long enough and it was the right time in my life to receive the help that I needed. I tried to prepare myself, to open up and also be open-minded, and let the therapist do what he or she needed to do with me during each session. But I knew deep down, this was only because I had been so closed off to it all, not accepting for so many years, that I really did need some help. CBT had been the perfect method of therapy for me at that time. I had done a bit of research before my sessions began, and I knew that it was there to create a different pattern within my brain. Its job was to train positive thoughts from the negative ones It was also there to help you focus on the now, the today rather than worry about the unknown future. Within my sessions, I had also learnt a very important lesson that CBT was not there to take away mental health issues, but there to teach you how to manage them. I had spent many years reading books on how to feel happy, how to feel less stressed, how to deal with anger but they just gave me advice. CBT was on a completely different level, as I had someone there to see everything from a whole other angle, giving me the tools and lessons that I had needed for so many years.

For so long, my negative thought patterns had cost me so many jobs, so many relationships and put me in such bad situations that could have been dealt with in a better way. I had been beating myself up for years, making myself so unhappy, and I just never had the tools to know what to do with those thoughts that took over my brain. It also cost me David once, and I didn't want it to happen again. I knew it was accepting that I had an issue was extremely hard but knowing how to cope with it was the real reward.

Turning up to my first session, I was torn between wanted to turn the other way but I also ready to sort myself out. I sat down in the waiting area with the same form I filled out at the doctors which asked me how I had been feeling the last two weeks.

Just as I finished my questionnaire, a young lady walked in and called my name. Her name was Esin and was from Argentina. She explained we would be having twelve sessions together and talked me through how she would help me. As I worried about having to drag up my childhood, I made my bum remain seated and when the first hour session ended, it felt like only ten minutes.

Parallel to starting my therapy, January was taking its time, and all I had was the wonder of who killed Lucy Beale in EastEnders. I had started another temp job where I would be helping out the manager with secretarial work for a private optician on the very well-known, prestigious Harley Street. As I walked along the prestigious street on my first day, dreading the long month that lay ahead, I imagined all the worst-case scenarios as I always dreaded the worst. The job itself may have consisted of smiling sweetly as they demanded their eye test, I also had the job of running up and down the FOUR flights of stairs, setting up meetings with heavy Pret platters and drinks, sneakily nibbling at the tuna and cucumber baguettes. Ending the day was franking literally up to 500 letters, all being recorded or made special delivery which took up hours. I was often cooped up alone in the post room with a guy from accounts, it wouldn't be so bad if he had just talked to me about normal things. Instead, I had to listen to the guy go on about how he wanted to go into the porn industry as he had; all the equipment', all the while trying not to stare at his oversized diamond earring that took over his left earlobe.

Because I got on with my boss, it obviously made the days bearable. He was open-minded to my quirky comments, he was approachable, and he let me leave early to go to other interviews. Being stuck in one office for a whole month and surviving it was an achievement in itself, but I was proud I lasted the entire time. I actually experienced my first 'last day' at a job. I had an actual goodbye! I'd even made friends with the boss and was even told I'd be missed! Me? Missed from the office? I was used to being escorted from the premises by security. It felt good not being fired for being me.

Every Monday, I had my hour at 6 pm with Esin. Knowing I was only given twelve meetings of CBT, I always felt pressure to achieve something after each session. But feeling nothing by the fifth, I felt frustrated. I had been given homework and write-ups to read each week, but I told her I was a 'doer'. I needed some kind of physical exercise to help me punch through my brick wall that had loomed over me for so many years. I was warned that during my sessions, my anxiety and stress levels could be heightened as feelings and emotions were rawer had suddenly surfaced. I had been extra emotional and even paranoid when I spent time with David. It was hard for anyone who didn't suffer from mental health issues to understand.

It wasn't until the sixth session when Esin and I did some physical exercises, when something finally happened to me. There was a sudden change in my brain, like she had unblocked part of my brain. She asked me to sit in a chair, which had an empty chair sat facing me in front of it. The empty chair had an imaginary version of my brain sitting in it. The imaginary brain was telling me all the things I had told myself over the years. I'm not good enough. No one wants me. No one will accept me. No one will stay with me. I'm a failure. I'm never going to be a success. If I marry, I'll only end up getting a divorce. I'm going to die a horrible death.

Esin asked me to tell my imaginary me to stop saying those things to me.

I was then told to sit in the imaginary me chair and ask out loud, "Why should I stop, Naomi? I like telling you these things."

I was then asked to go back to my original chair and say out loud, "Because it makes me feel bad and I don't want to feel this way, so STOP IT."

I sat back in the imaginary chair. The thoughts had stopped. Vanished. Nothing entered my head. It was a sense I had never experienced in my life. My brain, which was constantly flowing and forming negative thoughts, suddenly came to an immediate halt.

I cried from relief. I was beaming. Esin smiled at me with a tear in her eye, she looked at me with an expression of real achievement. We had broken a wall. The light was shining through a long dark tunnel I had been looking through all those years, some of the weight had been lifted.

It was all about practice. Getting into new routines and new ideas that were offered to me, which I had blocked from thinking myself. Learning from another person's perspective was incredible.

I was also set the 'two-minute challenge' which sounded so easy but when the mind is in a certain state, it's actually quite hard and needs practice. It's an exercise that forces you to focus on a mundane task rather than react to a thought or a feeling. Making a cup of tea, polishing a pair of shoes, picking up a newspaper to read, anything to take you away and relieve stress that's has built up over a short period of time. Those two minutes can change how to deal with bad decisions from unrealistic thoughts. I was learning that depression and anxiety was something I was going to live with, it was something that could potentially always be with me, but it was learning how to deal with it and control it which was key. I now had the tools to deal with it in a positive way that wasn't ruining my life.

A radical lesson I learnt during my time with Esin was not to explain myself to people and not to ask reassurance from unimportant people, especially in the work place. I have hated all of my uncreative, uninspiring jobs, but I still cared and continuously found myself explaining and defending myself which I didn't want to do anymore. It left me exhausted. I was paranoid that my strong personality would rub people up the wrong way, I didn't like the thought of annoying people, but I wanted to be myself too. I was constantly checking I had done the job right and always panicked if I was even two minutes late for work. But once I learnt to not care about those things daily and learnt not to care if someone wanted to pigeon hole me or judge me on my looks, I felt the stress lift off my chest I felt less paranoid and more relaxed. Of course, I knew that not everyone would warm to my strong opinions, my quirky ways and flamboyancy, but I learnt to not worry about that. I was starting to feel good.

Once my sessions were over, it was May, and I sent Esin a card to say thank you for her work. As hard as it was to experience those sessions, it really did change my outlook on so many things. The exercises she taught me had given me a new lease on life which I will forever be grateful. I knew that I wasn't fully 'cured' by any means, there were things that Esin couldn't do as I wasn't ready, and she wasn't qualified to tackle. Esin had explained to me with all the terrible things I witnessed as a child, plus the mental abuse I had suffered from Bill and being thrown out, I had been suffered from post-traumatic stress and I didn't even know it. The nightmares I had suffered all my life and the anxiety I suffered was all part and parcel of post trauma that needed to be looked at and different form of therapy called psychotherapy helped with that. Esin advised that I should be referred again in the future to receive psychotherapy which would really dig deep into my past and help me accept and let go of my childhood, but like CBT, I had to be ready for it myself.

It was a few days before my birthday and David told me he was off to Chicago for a work trip. I was gutted! Not only was David going to miss my birthday, he was off to the land where we would be able to see Povs! But then he gave me a card to open. It was a note telling me once his work event was over, he was going to fly me over to Chicago to come meet him and we would stay with Povs. It was all arranged. I was ecstatic and felt very lucky indeed.

Seeing Povs again was fantastic, and David and Povs got on really well and we spent the four days we had together. We went for walks, had lunches out, went to some fun bars and generally had a great time. Whilst in each other's company, Povs and I arranged to go to Ibiza together. It was something we had talked about for years, so it was long overdue. But before any trip of Ibiza could happen, David and I had some fun that turned out a little different to what was planned...

Throughout my life, I was considered to be one of the most strong-minded, pig-headed people that my friends and family had ever met. I was as determined as they come; if I didn't want to do something, I simply wouldn't do it. No matter what people did or said to try and sway me. And if I said that I would do something, I would go out of my way to make it happen and saw it through to the end. After 32 years of never smoking, never trying a single drug or even being curious about drugs, due to my parents' addictions, I had been adamant throughout my entire life that I would never try anything. I was just too scared and kept my mind closed. People's persuasions never tempted me, nothing made me interested, and no desire to experience anything entered my head. It wasn't until I had a spontaneous, outrageous, out of nowhere idea to try Ecstasy.

Summer was gazing down on London and it was festival season again. June 13th and Field Day music festival had arrived. David and I had had so much fun there in 2014, we had to go back. We headed there with some of David's workmates, and planned to consume too much cider and dance in the tents, as we had done the previous year.

Chilling for the best part of the day, and I was feeling restless and wanted a dance. Whenever I heard great music, I couldn't help but move. The DJ Ten Walls was on in the tent next to us, famous for its track *Walking with Elephants*. We had been sitting around in the sun long enough. Swallowing the sounds and beats, and letting them take over my body, I suddenly felt compelled to do something very out of character. David's friend Ed had taken two pills of Ecstasy, I didn't even know it was called 'dropped' when you took pills. Ed's usual forward-facing eyes had turned him into the comedian Marty Feldman, with one eyeball looking in a different direction to the other, but for some random bizarre reason, I suddenly wanted to try it. David had never done it either and with Ed wanting to leave early, David and I suddenly had half a pill each in our hands. David asked if I was sure about this and for a second, I asked myself what I was doing. But I was ready to open mind up to something because it was on my terms with no pressure. I looked down at the yellow-peachy tint of a spotted half a tablet and prepared myself. David couldn't believe after so many years of me adamant that I would never try a drug, I was about to jump from a pint of cider, to a class A ecstasy pill. It was also an experience we were about to have for the first time and share together. While I was building myself up to take the half a pill, *Walking with Elephants* started to play, and I remember the tune in my mind so clearly as David calmly swallowed his half and right there and then. So, with a swig of my warm cider, I took mine too. We were about to embark on a whole-new experience.

Half an hour later, David and I were in the tent, and with the DJ had really kicked into his set, but my pill hadn't. I wasn't feeling anything apart from disappointment, and David was the same. But then it happened, 45 minutes in. A wave of what I can only describe as softness through my body and a tingling sensation that started at my toes and my fingers, that moved quickly up my body to the tip of my head. I had the feeling as though I was floating upwards, but with my feet still firmly on the ground and completely in control. The lights became brighter and the music became clearer. Any thought of panic or worry on what was going to happen had completely vanished. As I danced to the beat and felt the warm sensation ran through my body, David was suddenly behaving hilariously, hugging me, hugging strangers, telling me he loved me, telling strangers he loved them. I had never really noticed the effects ecstasy had on people until I was actually aware of it. It had opened my eyes up to a whole new world, and it was very friendly!

David and I had five festivals booked that year, including seeing *The Who* in Hyde Park. The novelty of taking Ecstasy was fresh and we planned to take mere half a pill each for each occasion. Our second festival that summer was LoveBox to see *Rudimental*. We met up with David's friend Ed again, who found our new pill-taking escapade almost endearing that we 32 and 33, and fresh to the world of taking this recreational drug. As David and I took our shared pill for only the second time in our lives, Ed knocked back just one rather than two he had at Field Day. We all danced until the sun went down before David and I went to the LoveBox after party to see Groove Armada where we got hold of MDMA which we knew was similar to Ecstasy. Dabbing our little fingers into the small plastic bag, we both tasted, for the first time, the incredibly bitter taste it gave off. Within 45 minutes, I was walking around the club positive that there was a bubble machine blowing large bubbles into the room. While Groove Amada played and everyone danced, I must have looked rather bizarre trying to pop what I thought was one giant bubble. There was no bubble machine and no bubbles. I was hallucinating. I could only assume that the MDMA has something else added to it. It felt amazing and was in complete control while I enjoyed my imaginary bubbles. At this point, David was in a seriously deep conversation with a guy who was nodding along and looked as though they were talking about a riveting subject. It turned out they were talking about work and measurements, graphics and past projects This drug had some hilarious effects on us.

After that summer of love, my new motto in life was NEVER SAY NEVER. From being so adamant about something and then being open to try it, made me realise anything could happen in life.

August had come around quickly, and Edinburgh Festival had fallen upon all the comics. All the usual questions were appearing on Facebook—which venue do you have? How many weeks are you there for? Have you done your flyers? Have you sorted your accommodation?

I, on the other hand, had decided to do the Camden Fringe Comedy Festival that year. A smaller fringe to Edinburgh, but no less exciting. I had heard some wonderful things about the Camden festival, so was happy to be a part of it. When I was accepted and given a fabulous venue at the Etcetera Theatre, I was unaware of one fundamental thing that was very different to the Edinburgh fringe; I was told I had to price my own show! This was tricky because I had put a lot of thought into my second show, but I still have little self-worth to even think to price the hours' worth of comedy to anything pricy. So, I placed the tickets at £5 each. I was scared no one would turn up if I priced them any higher.

My solo show was coming up and I had a section of my show to fill with material. All I wanted to do for so long was physical comedy. I had a well-practised section where I talked about being back in a relationship, as my first solo show heavily featured around being single. When David and I first got together, WhatsApp wasn't around, and Facebook had been enough hassle when we broke up. Once everyone was using WhatsApp, for a long time was nothing more than a messaging device for me, merely another way of contacting friends or loved ones. But for anyone in a new relationship, I felt for them. WhatsApp had a tendency to make anyone go a little nuts…

You send him a message—one tick. He has received it—two ticks. He has read it—Blue ticks. You can see he is online. Nothing. He goes offline. Frustration and insecurity kicks in.

You wonder, because he read the message, why didn't he reply? It wasn't like the old texts, when you got that 'has received' note pop up. You never knew if it had been read though! WhatsApp is a dangerous thing. Even staying online makes no difference if they have read it, thanks to the blue tick scheme that came in not too long ago.

So, you find yourself staring at your phone, checking to see if and when he comes back online. There he is again! But still no 'typing' is seen on your screen and no reply pops-up. Agitation and vivid images take over the mind.

You question if you should send another message. Then you remind yourself, you are still showing that best version of yourself, you don't want to start sending more messages on top of the already read messages, because it's then, and only then, the crazy intense side begin to show!

You go to bed, have one last check on WhatsApp and see they were online only a few minutes ago, but STILL no reply! You wonder who they could be was talking to, so, you find yourself just going online, not even going to talk to anyone else, just looking, leering, hoping the person in question will come back online and start typing! Next thing you know, you are finding yourself setting your alarm clock at 4am and going online, staring at the phone, slipping slowly into madness, knowing they are offline sleeping but desperately hoping when they wake up to see you were online so they start wondering who you might have been talking to at that time of night and wait and wonder even more when they will finally message back, and when they finally do, the sheer relief that you know they are still interested is the best feeling in the world... Madness. Exhausting, pointless, chaotic madness.

Even when years later and into my own relationship, I would get that blood-boiling, frustrating, unloved feeling when I see my boyfriend had read my message but not answered. One tick, two ticks, blue ticks. I started to take this story and add it into my sets in the comedy clubs, and I had lost count how many women and some men from the audience who came to tell me how they could relate so much to my annoyance. Once I tried this set a few times, I had incorporated my relatable WhatsApp theory into the show.

Whilst getting the last few bits together, booking my preview in London and having my photo taken for the poster, I should not have been thinking about holidays. But Povs and I decided to book a last-minute flight to Ibiza. Even though at the time I was in bed with a stinking hangover and vowed never to drink again, I was excited to book the flights. After all those times we had planned to go, it was time! So, a month before my solo show was on, all I could think about were the hot beaches and amazing clubs and what outfits to wear each night. And of course, the company I'd be in. I couldn't wait to see Povs again. She planned a couple of days in London first, so my partner in crime, the crazy American comedian, would be back to cause fun and mayhem. The day before heading to Ibiza, I thought it would be a great idea to have a relaxing treat. David had bought me a Groupon voucher for my birthday which I had saved, so using it before the holiday seemed liked the perfect idea. I turned up to a very tiny clinic in North London, with only a little old man to greet me at the door. He asked me what my problem was; "Nothing," I answered.

"Then why are you here?" he asked, looking confused. I explained I had been bought the voucher as a birthday present and I was just there to use it. His facial expression turned from confused to amused. David hadn't booked a message in a spa or a facial at a beauty salon, I was standing in clinic that specialised in Chinese acupuncture.

He told me he would be performing a procedure called 'cupping' on my back. I had no idea what this was, and he asked where I wanted it.

"In the massage room, if that's OK," I replied nervously. He meant which body part. "Oh... My back?"

He took me to a tiny room where I was told to strip off. Fully to my knickers. I suddenly felt trapped, uncomfortable and awkward. I was then told to put my face into the hole on the massage table and try and relax. As the sound of drilling and builders shouting went on outside the next to the window, relaxing was the last thing I could do. After acupuncture needles were placed down my entire back and neck, the man started the 'cupping'. It felt like I was receiving love bites that left perfectly circular shaped bruises for over a week. For the 30 minutes I was left to 'relax', while the drills carried on outside and the cups still sucked on my back, the little man kept knocking on the door every five minutes, asking me how I was feeling. I felt as relaxed as a someone with dental phobia sitting in a dentist's chair covered in leeches with a drill on full speed next to their head. What felt like a lifetime of 'back sucking', the session was up to have the cups removed and my bruises were revealed. I never went back again and vowed to never be 'cupped' again.

When Povs had arrived in the UK, we had a big night out in London ready for our trip to Ibiza. With hardly any sleep and still pretty drunk from the night before, we got our flight to Ibiza after all those years of talking about it. Once we landed, we spent five days drinking cocktails, dancing until the early hours of the morning, relaxed on the beach and caused havoc like we always did together. The novelty of Ecstasy hadn't worn for me, and without realising how easy it was to find something I hadn't gone out looking for before, I was suddenly given dusty pink pills that were served to me on a mini silver saucer like a side salad in the back room of a bar. On our third night in gorgeous Ibiza, Povs and I danced through the night to Paul Van Dyke in Amnesia and ended up at an after-party. There, in the middle of the room was a tall round table, and on this table was a gigantic bag of MDMA, just sitting there on offer for anyone who wanted it. I couldn't help but dive in as I felt like a young child who had first tasted candy. Ibiza was a seriously hard danced, fun fuelled, energy filled dance fest of amazing memories. And Povs and I told each other that we would return one day.

Returning home from Ibiza and I had really missed David. We had decided to move in together, so once I was back in London, we went on the hunt for a little flat for the two of us. Mentally, I wasn't in a good place. Taking so many Ecstasy pills and rounds of MDMA every day for five days for the first time in my life, left me feeling very odd. I was experiencing my first ever come down and spent many days later crying wishing I could still be dancing with Povs in our own Ibiza bubble.

Ten days later, David and I had moved into our new flat in Holloway, and my comedown had melted away. I had joked that once me and David moved back in with each other, I would get a kitten as it was something I had longed for. David had tried to put his foot down as the flat wasn't allowed pets, plus he thought it was too much of a responsibility. But each day, as we unpacked and made our flat our home, I knew a kitten was what was missing.

On the third Saturday in August, David was off for a morning run and I sneaked off to view six kittens in Notting Hill. As I gazed around the six babies in awe of them all, there sat a seven-week-old boy, with shiny black fur, slightly larger than the other kittens. He was sitting comfortably on a patchwork cushion that lay on a rocking chair. As he looked up at me with confidence, he was so beautiful as the sun shone down on his tiny body. Then I spied a tiny black and white kitten, running across the room that caught my attention. She was amongst two other adorable tiny kittens that lay peacefully in the sun, but this little female cat, with her tiny legs running under the coffee table, made me chose her. As I picked her up, she had the tiniest most pathetic little meow. I knew I wanted her there and then. By the time I had travelled back home, David was already back from his run. He saw the little cardboard box I had taken to collect her in was closed and with my smile, he knew we had a new addition to the family.

Like anything new, adjustments had to be made. Getting to know our new cat, learning what kind of personality she had and choosing her name took some time. We thought about calling her Cilla, with her jet-black coat and with national treasure, Cilla Black, we grew up watching, had recently passed, so it seemed like the perfect name. But it didn't quite fit and was left nameless for days, with other names not quite feeling right. It wasn't until the following weekend on a Saturday morning we found the perfect name. As she was so tiny, she couldn't climb onto the bed on her own. So, lifting her up with one hand, she started to explore the space on the bed. And there she found my morning unwashed armpits that had a stench of BO. And right there and then, our tiny kitten started to lick my armpits. Could we really call her BO? Bo? Bobo! That was it, she was named.

Over the next few weeks, we noticed Bobo's personality wasn't like any other cats. She behaved much more like a dog. Cats sleep, eat, play, jump well, purr and give you attention when they want something. Our cat was horrendous at jumping like a cat can do so graciously. Instead, started to bring us anything stick-like in her mouth, and would leave it in our laps to throw again and again. Her favourite thing to play fetch with was the glow sticks we were given at raves. Our first trip to the vets we bought Bobo a travel bag, and we were surprised as she just walked into it, no hassle, no struggle. Once on the train, I thought it was only fair to let Bobo out of the bag and sit her on my lap. I felt nervous, knowing it was her first time out of the flat and we didn't know what to expect. As we were sitting on a four-seater over ground train, I placed her on the spare seat next to me. And like no other cat I had seen, she just curled up and stayed sat there, minding her own business. Other passengers walked by, some didn't believe what they had seen, others stopped to say, "That's a cat!" She was a dog actually, trapped inside a cat's body.

Nerves covered my whole body, as I stood alone waiting for the opening music to start the beginning of my show, Bonnie Tyler's, *I Need a Hero*. As much as my stomach was churning, my face, staring back at myself in the small changing room mirror in the green room, looked calm. I was just about to go onstage to perform my second solo show. As soon as the track started to play, my comic announcement began. A comedian on the circuit, A J Roberts was a master of impressions, so as a favour, he recorded my announcement with the voice of the narrator from X Factor, introducing me onto the stage. Before I knew it, I was dancing onto the theatre floor, wearing a huge strap on penis around my waist and an oversized smile on my face. The audience were clapping along and enjoying my absurd moves, while I thrust my plastic penis to slap the faces of my chosen victims. I made sure even though I wasn't doing any particular dance routine, I danced with as much energy as I could.

The interesting thing about my 2015 show was, there were parts to it that were completely untested, however, I knew wholeheartedly, they would be the most successful parts. This was because they weren't the usual 'jokes' I had chosen to add in my favourite form of comedy, physical comedy. Growing up with the likes of Norman Wisdom, Mr Bean Bottom and Fawlty Towers, I was in love with visual physical comedy more than straight jokes. I was confident the physical comedy I was going to bring to my show was going to be successful because, in some respects, physical comedy and slapstick had always been the easiest form of comedy to perform. I had the guts to look stupid, the timing and I could convey a story though my body and facial expressions. I had wanted to perform physical comedy in the comedy clubs, but it was difficult due to the space of some of the tiny stages and the short five-minute time frame I was given for each open mic set. So, it never became more than an idea or a vision. It wasn't until my second show, I knew I had the resources and the time to show off my skill.

The first section of physical comedy I wanted to add to the show was inspired from seeing so many gym work out routines and the idea that there were so many working mums who wanted to stay fit too. I had the idea of my gym workout routine going completely wrong. I chose the Eric Prydze song *Call on me* that people recognised as work out music. I burned it onto a CD and purposely made the tune get faster and faster. But I needed a reason for this. Drugs. Cocaine, to be exact. I hadn't tried it myself, but I found the concept of me performing a gym routine, looking like I was on drugs hilarious.

Before I knew it, I was standing on stage, pretending to snort what the audience was to believe was cocaine. It was in fact flour. My comedy moment was that I told the audience I didn't know how much cocaine I was meant to snort, so I had a huge pile of it on a coaster and just shoved the whole lot in my face, temporarily blinding myself and covering the front row with flour too. As the audience got to enjoy the mess and the chaos, *Call on Me* began to play. So, whilst holding a plastic baby, pretending it was a real one I began my workout whilst being a working mother in the modern world. I started the workout routine calm and sensible while I held the baby in my arms. Of course, the music began to get faster and faster to represent the cocaine kicking in. The music got so fast my legs couldn't keep up and were all over the place, leaving me to throw the baby into the audience and my facial expressions showing utter inanity and chaos with the flour still flying from my face too. The audience loved it and I felt completely and utterly comfortable doing what I was doing,

After some jokes I had written about my love for Big Macs, I decided to incorporate an actual Big Mac into my show. I had the idea of serenading my favourite burger which would be placed in its box in the middle of the stage. The lights would shine low, a disco ball would start up, and Bonnie Tyler's *Total Eclipse of the Heart* would start playing, creating an overly romantic moment between myself and the burger. With no practise at all, during my live show, I started to eat the burger with so much passion that I was almost snogging it, making the burger smear all over my face. While the love song became more powerful, the burger moved from my face, down my neck and all over the tiny gym top I had changed into for the previous scene.

I may have stank of Big Mac at the end of the show, but I was pretty proud of the hour I had performed. Of course, me being me, I felt sad after it was all over, wondering what it would be like to be going to a theatre every night to perform physical comedy for people. But it was over, and I had to now find a 'proper' job again.

I did receive a wonderful review that really did surprise me. A comedy reviewer called View from the Gods had come to see me without me even knowing.

Review – View from the Gods

"Naomi Hefter certainly knows how to make an entrance. Bursting onto the stage with enthusiasm, confetti and some rather interesting clothing decisions, she makes clear from the get-go that she's no shrinking violet. If you're not one of those people who respond well to audience participation, this is going to be a hellish kind of gig for you. If, however, you're up for a bit of craic, then you'll find Hefter's foul-mouthed, opinionated style wildly funny—she's not to everyone's taste, certainly not tasteful, but many (myself included) will find her a real riot. Appropriate then, that she's named her solo show

Chaos; there's absolutely nothing serene about her personality or material.

"Hefter claims that her show is based on real things that happened to her, and there certainly are some anecdotes which get so many easy laughs of recognition (one tick, two ticks, blue ticks), that you can well believe this. Her observational comedy is chosen well and used sparingly. Other stories, however, are so outrageous that you begin to think if Hefter is in fact telling the truth, you're not quite sure whether to run away and hide or buy her a vodka and salute her as a hero.

"Hefter is the devilish voice we've all heard at some point telling us to do something we really shouldn't, but the difference is, she does as she says. If we're not happy at work, we should leave, she tells us. Well, she's taken that advice herself on many occasions. Having been fired more times than years she's spent on the planet, Hefter is fearless, resilient and whimsical, which fits quite well into her current role as a performer.

"Over the course of 50 minutes, Hefter covers boyfriends, bad jobs and Big Macs, always with plenty of commitment to her jokes. She's certainly unafraid of making a fool of herself, in order to nail a punch line, and never reluctant to put the effort in. Not only does this show come with plenty of gags, it also features poetry readings and a fitness workout. How's that for extra value? We're lovin' it. Hefter whizzes through her far-fetched yet apparently true tales at a cracking pace, but also demonstrates the power of silence in a gloriously funny sequence involving a bit of Bonnie Tyler and a disco ball.

"Honestly, if Hefter rocked up at my office claiming to be the new temp, I don't know how I'd react. Mainly with trepidation. If there were any magazines lying around with wax samples, I'd definitely hide those. (Don't ask.) However, if I spotted Hefter's name on the line up for a comedy gig, I'd be there like a shot. She's part Hungarian, pure filth, and totally hilarious."

After hunting for yet another 'day job', I was offered a temp job working as a secretary for a 'mystery' company where I didn't need an interview. I accepted there and then, and was incredibly curious where this mystery job could be, but also prepared myself for anything to come my way, with the luck I had with temp jobs, September 7th, on my first day, I was given the address and told I was looking forward to doing a job where I could use my writing skills instead of my 'waiting for the phone to ring' skills. I turned up to a grand building in Holborn and asked security where to go for my first day. I didn't even have a company name, just a contact of Kerry. Security told me to turn right and head down a corridor. I ended up in a giant old-fashioned room that had been decked out with huge bright lights and giant posters reading LONDON FASHION WEEK. Models were wandering around with flasks of coffee, wearing fascinating garments of shimmer and glitz that were being pinned on by people. It was then I suddenly realised I had been sent to the wrong place. I went back to security where they told me they thought I was a model and sent me to the studio where the catwalk had been built for the week. I should have taken it as a huge compliment, but I actually felt deflated and sad knowing that I wasn't going to be part of something so creative and inspiring, I had been completely mistaken for one thing, when I was actually, I was something quite the opposite. A temp who was stuck in a job rut, continuously feeling like a failure and would probably be fired from this job too. When Kerry came to pick me up and showed me my seat and I was explained my role. I was working for the Masons. The famous Freemasons with the secret handshake and the unknown curious meetings. I had heard only of the peculiar group but had no idea what they were, who they were or what they did.

Within the first ten minutes, I quickly Googled them and still had no idea what it all meant. But within a matter of days, I certainly got the gist of it all. My job was a most unusual one. I was asked start by reading through hundreds upon hundreds of application forms and letters from people all over the world, wanting to become a Mason. I didn't realise how popular it was and how much people wanted to be part of it. My job was to then email all the people back who weren't allowed to join. This included anyone from the Middle East and parts of Africa, homosexuals and women. I couldn't quite believe these backwards rules still applied in 2015. Within days into the job, with my name Naomi Hefter at the end of each email, I was beginning to receive the most bizarre replies. Some begging me to let them join and if it were up to me. Some replied telling me, if I didn't let them in, aliens would invade the earth or the world would end. Others personally messaging me through Facebook telling me God had personally spoke to the applicant and told them they had been chosen to become a Mason. It got really bad when I was receiving death threats on my Facebook from people from the Far East. Photos of machine guns from men in Syria and Afghanistan, telling me they knew my name and where I worked. When I told Kerry about what I had been receiving, she calmly replied, "Oh, don't worry, I get death threats all the time, but the glass here is gun and bomb proof, so nothin' to worry about love." Was I meant to feel reassured now? I was genuinely scared so without even asking, I changed my name on my applicant responses to Naomi Jenkins, the girl who became my alter ego. There was only one Naomi Hefter on Facebook to message, but there were over fifty Naomi Jenkins.

Each day, while I sent these emails, I heard an organ being played during the Masons' Lodge meetings. I had seen the room they attended and not only was the room vast and grand, but at the front sat three huge gold thrones. Every time the organ played, I had visions of people turning up dressed in robes and masks like Tom Cruise in *Eyes Wide Shut*, having strange kinky sex.

I had been temping at the Masons for three months, wondering every day when I was going to be assassinated by a rejected applicant. The money was very low and to be honest, it was a very tedious job emailing people that same thing every day and receiving abusive replies. I just remember feeling… lost. How was I meant to get out of this rut? Job agencies were calling me to check if I was looking for work and one day, I decided to take one of the calls just in case there was a better paid, permanent job on offer that didn't involve reception work. I had been applying for low paid intern writing jobs but didn't think for one minute I would get one because of the competition. On the other end of the line was a pleasant-sounding lady who I recognised the voice of. Bearing in mind I had met easily 100 recruiters over the last five years, so placing a face to the voice was tricky. She sounded excited about a full time permanent, well-paid job that was perfect for me. I was immediately interested as I asked for more information. It was to work as a receptionist—for Rolex. Not only was I being asked to work for a company I had already worked for, but also been fired from back in 2009. I had to think on my feet for a reason NOT to go for the interview.

"Um, I can't go for this role, I am against working for a company that charges ridiculous prices for watches." Why couldn't I just have said I was off on holiday for three weeks or something believable like a normal person?

I couldn't believe it. I had worked for that many companies in London, they had run out of places for me to work. I decided enough was an enough. I needed to pull myself out of the temp reception rut. I realised I needed to wake up knowing I had a good day ahead of me. I knew I needed to do something worthwhile and decent. So, I made a list of all my strengths and created a list of jobs I could do well. Entertaining, engaging with people, talking, communicating, writing, creating, meeting people, networking and bringing out confidence in people. I also made a list of all the things, and all the jobs, and all of the aspects of those jobs I hated. Uniforms, ridiculous rules, office politics, sucking up to people, being given mindless tasks to do, not using my creative skills, waiting for the phone to ring, getting the tube at 8:30 am to a place I didn't want to go to and being around people that weren't on my wave length.

That weekend, David and I went for a walk, and I told him about the phone call about Rolex and how much it upset me. He randomly came up with an idea for what I could do for a new business I could set up on my own. To be a theatre and comedy tour guide around London. No more offices, no more judgemental people, no more mundane duties. Just me, entertaining the general public and talking to them about subjects I liked to talk about.

So, while I stayed at the Masons, I decided my first job was to so some research. Who were my competitors? Who were my target audience? Which places hadn't been covered that I could talk about? I also went headfirst and contacted a web designer to set up a page to promote my tours, as I didn't have a clue what I was doing. Then I was to set the huge task to myself of researching all the information, the history, the facts, the stories, you name it. Theatres, The West End, the musicals, the plays, the comedy clubs, the present shows, the history, the myths, the legends, the facts, the dates, anything to make this tour incredibly insightful and fun to be on, plus adding my own comic twist on it all. I literally just stuck right in and got on with it every single day.

Realistically, I thought it would take about six months to put together. I set myself a goal to work towards and a date in mind, March 26, 2016. Within days, I made hundreds of notes on little cards, slowing putting together a script for my 90-minute tour. Once I had written out the script, I had the task of learning it all off by heart. I was really proud of myself, considering I soaked up so much information in such a short amount of time. I felt positive about my new venture and was looking forward to 2016. There was one small problem, 2016 wasn't going to start off like I had hoped.

2016

Death and Love

When the Paris terrorist attacks tragically happening in November, 2015, they were still being talked about in January 2016 and rightly so. People in and around London were on edge. Warning signs were whirling, police were patrolling, and the news was telling the general public to be more vigilant. While armed police were guarding the underground tube entrances every day for extra safety, people were just waiting for the next ISIS attack. It wasn't the best of beginnings for a year and I woke up several nights in a row suffering from horrendous nightmares about terrorist attacks and death.

On January 10th the news had very quickly spread that the remarkable talent of David Bowie had passed away. He had been suffering from pancreatic cancer and had chosen not to tell the media. Walking though Brixton only a few days later to see the endless number of flowers and posters that had been laid down along Tunstall Road where he had a memorial painted years before, was now a huge shrine to the artist. Hundreds of photos, drawings and letters surrounded around the famous street art that is of David's face.

Days later, my grandma rang me to break the news that Aunty Tracey had been diagnosed with the same cancer. As Uncle Joe and Tracey literally lived in the middle of nowhere, she had just left pains she had been suffering from to run their course, hoping they would go away. Uncle Joe had repeatedly asked her to go to the doctor, but she never did. After leaving it too long and eventually having to go to hospital because the pains were so bad, she was told she had pancreatic cancer. She was given the catastrophic news that she had only 18 months left to live if she decided to have treatment.

Tracey wrote to me through Facebook telling me she had decided to go for chemotherapy and was feeling confident about it. Only three weeks later, she wrote to me again and her tone was different. She was telling me how proud she was of me and how she hoped I was happy. I knew something wasn't right, but I never let what could happen enter my head. I refused to believe anything bad could happen. My grandma rang me up at the beginning of March. Tracey's body hadn't taken to the chemotherapy and the cancer had taken over her body. She died the previous day with my cousins and doctor around her bed, laying in Uncle Joe's arms. With the thoughts and nightmares I had suffered from for so many years about death, I just went into shut down. I literally refused to believe it. The thought of death had disturbed me, and I didn't know how to accept. So, when I was told this news about my Aunty, I just simply didn't take it in. it was as though what I heard down the phone wasn't real...

Everyone was talking about a Netflix series called *Making a Murderer*. I didn't have a clue what it was about, but when I learnt it was a real-life crime documentary, I was very interested. Just like mine and David's intriguing obsession with *Forensic Files*, we eagerly sat to watch *Making a Murderer*. We finished the entire series in one sitting. Like many other viewers who watched, I was emotionally moved by this popular series and the two people it focused on. As I watched the 17-year-old Brendan Dassey being sent to life in prison, for something I really believed he didn't do, I felt empathy and sorrow towards this boy. He was genuine and had a gentle poise about him. There were so many other people who also believed his innocence, so protests were being made to release him and online signed petitions were everywhere. I decided to do my bit so I wrote him a hand-written letter, telling him what I thought of the show and that I could see he was innocent. I was so pleasantly surprised but also shocked when less than two weeks later, I received a letter back from him. And over the next nine months, we wrote to each other every two weeks. I would inform him about how the show was getting great positive feedback, and I would tell him about my life in London. His letters were fascinating with his stories on the

159

inside and tales about other inmates. Overall, Brendan stressed to me that he just to keep his head down, get his situation sorted, and one day hopefully lead a normal life with his family and eventually, find someone to love.

Spring had come early, the web designers who I approached about my walking tour business had also made a Twitter, Facebook and Google page, making sure my website was high up on the SEO. It was slowly coming together, apart from two things, marketing and business. I knew nothing about either. And a new business with no business experience was making me panic. Promoting my solo comedy show in Edinburgh with a flyer and a smile was one thing, but setting up the promotion and marketing of this new business venture and possible career, was a whole different ball game.

When I had handed out my flyers in Edinburgh, punters knew I was merely trying to bring in a crowd. Customers were all there for comedy and they were always interested by passionate enthusiastic promoters. I had filled my 100-seater room back in 2013 every single day no problem. But flyering an unknown brand-new business, a walking tour of the West-End business no less, people often turned their heads away at me as they walked through the streets of London. And when I did catch the attention of some people, they actually thought I was nothing more than a girl promoting a new fun thing for a new tour guide on the scene. I found myself with that familiar feeling creep up on me again, when I had started stand-up comedy. The assumptions people had made about me. Trying to open people's minds that I might be that person there to entertain. I was just the girl help promote the tour for the business owner. I found the promoting my business was suddenly a full-time job in itself, explaining that I was going to be their tour guide and getting people on board. I wasn't even sure who I was meant to be promoting me and my business to. I knew as much about marketing as I did about business.

I had spent days flyering to people that weren't interested in such a niche. I knew I had to get my tour in places people would see it and would be interested in it. Time Out magazine. I also thought of quirky theatres and bars. I dropped by cafes and little shops around Soho, pubs and anywhere that had a notice board or a place to leave flyers. More importantly, I thought about approaching quirky Londoners who would be interested in such a quirky idea. But quirky Londoners didn't want to go to the touristy expensive West End, they were all in the East End amongst the street art and vintage shops. I was feeling so frustrated, three weeks had past and I had only done one tour. For what it was worth, they loved the tour, and I was also reviewed for Time Out magazine, and did a double page spread about me and the unique tour I offered;

"Stand-up comedian Naomi Hefter leads this tour through Theatreland with quick fire impersonations and quizzes, the winners of which get to walk away with packets of Palma Violets. Offering a solid mix of theatre facts and West End fables—tales of gay ghosts, theatrical superstitions and arson all featured—Hefter peppers the route with cameos from productions past and present. With a quick dive into her handbag, she reappears as Hugh Jackman playing Jean Valjean in Les Mis, another rustle in the bottomless bag and she is Erik from Phantom of the Opera. The impressions could be longer and bigger, not least because the response of passing shoppers, tourists and beleaguered West End workers really adds to the fun. Though not as polished as the shows it is a tribute to, Walking the West End will leave you armed with theatre trivia that'll wow even your most luvvie-ish pals."

But one spread wasn't enough and writing to other websites that promoted free and cheap things to do in London was hard. I had written to newspapers, magazines and endless websites but heard nothing back.

With blood, sweat and a lot of tears, setting up a business was doing just that to me. And I was starting to resent it. The fun of the job was very quickly deteriorating. With no money and no bookings, I had started to question if it was worth all of the hassle, but then I didn't want to go back to a reception job. I wanted to make something of myself from my own back. I was torn. My comedy gigs had taken a backseat, I hadn't written for weeks, and quality time with David had been pushed aside being so consumed and preoccupied in trying to make the tours work. With stacks of flyers now cluttering the living room floor, it was now my life and it was up to me to make it work. I was going out each day walking for miles promoting and handing out flyers and just like in 2009 when I was job hunting, I was dropping weight again and was feeling very low. I cried every single day at the rejection I felt took over and those familiar lost and deflated demons consumed me again. My CBT exercises had gone out of the window as I felt like biggest failure and a stupid naive idiot who thought this could even work. After spending three days in bed, I dragged myself out because this time, David was there to give me a hug and tell me it would be OK in the end.

Eight weeks had passed in and I was running very low on money and enthusiasm. One Monday morning with still no work coming my way, I was so disheartened and frustrated by it all, I didn't get up. If someone had picked up my flyer and showed up, I wasn't going to be there, and I didn't care. I knew no one would have shown. I felt like a failure. I felt like a defeatist I just lay in bed, falling into my dark hole again of wondering and thinking so many thoughts. Drifting in and out of sleep, often waking up and shutting out my negative thoughts before falling back to sleep again. I was starting to shut the world away once again. I had no booked gigs, I hadn't written, and then something entered my thoughts, was this the same pattern as before, a good thing that could change my life for the better and I was pushing it away? Was I really truly open to starting and having my own business? Did I love and believe in myself that this was going to work and be a success?

Two more weeks had gone by and I found myself in an incredibly dark state of my mind. No money, no bookings, no job and no ability to think positively. And I was fed up of taking Citalopram. I wallowed, I wept, I verbally kicked myself down further and completely stopped believing in myself. Depression was seeping back into my brain. Before I knew it, I was giving up on the tours and looked for another job I knew I was going to hate, plus I found myself shoplifting again. A pair of shoes here, a pair of jeans there, expensive makeup and some more perfume I didn't need. My drug was giving me my short-term fix once again.

All I wanted to do was to inspire people. Too many people hated their job. Too many people complained about their job.

Too many people stuck in a rut, bored of routine. Tired of the 9–5, sitting behind a computer screen doing a job they have no passion for and being reminded of all the things they want to achieve in life. Another week had passed, and I got a call from a job agency asking if I wanted to work for a company that was literally a 12-minute walk away from where I lived. I felt I had to take the opportunity even though it was yet another job I had no interest in. I would be in a car showroom working as a host. When I turned up for my interview, I did manage to show enthusiasm and somehow found a grain of positivity and told myself I was going to get the job, and I did. The company held just fifty people, and word had soon got around about my comedy. Luckily, most people were welcoming and positive. It was only two or three months in, I was beginning to regret taking the job and not sticking to the tours. The same pattern was happening with a few of the staff making remarks about my quirky ways. When I told people I wanted to be an author, a couple of the sales guys would laugh, telling me I had no chance of doing anything other than reception. Why couldn't I have just laughed back? I was getting cold feet working another uninspiring job again. The money wasn't bad and I needed it after so much time trying to make the tours work. Like any time in my life where I had started a new place, whether it was school, college or university, it would take about four or five months when 99% of people around me would get used to my eccentricity and finally warm to me. Showing my softer side helped but I didn't let people see that side of me for a while. On a night out, one of the sales guys had told me he didn't know what to think of me when I first started. He thought I had been purposely employed to come in and shake up the place like a glitter bomb that had exploded in the showroom. The reality was, I was just a new member of staff and I was just being myself. But I smiled and took what he said as a compliment.

The summer of 2016 had been blazing hot for weeks, and I started to get calls from the general public enquiring about my tours. But even with the work I put in to construct them, I had let them go. David and I had planned and booked a road trip from the North to the South West coast of Croatia come July. It was an incredible break away, with Hideout music festival taking place, we partied hard and relaxed even harder after. I didn't want it to end, but after 18 days away, we were missing Bobo, London and our own bed. When we returned, I was feeling good and more positive within myself so I thought it was a good time to stop taking Citalopram permanently. I felt it had run its course and I didn't feel the need to take it anymore. I was determined to come off it altogether, but I knew I had to be careful. It was strongly advised that the medication had to be weaned off bit by bit. In 2014 I had lowered my dose to 10mg from 20mg a day for a few weeks, then started to only take it every other day rather than every day. Unfortunately, I hadn't consulted with my doctor and I suddenly started to feel very peculiar. I felt like I was drunk and almost not part of the room. My thoughts were clouded and detached and found myself feeling incredibly paranoid. It was almost like a giant comedown from this legal medication. I felt disappointed with myself as I started to take it again to feel better. So two years later, by the month of August 2016, I really felt like it was time to stop all together. I just didn't want it in my life any longer. Plus, I wanted to try and use the skills I had learned from my CBT course when I got those negative feeling and thoughts in my head. I was extra careful to take lower doses for longer and not to skip any like last time. But the feelings came back again, and I felt very odd. I was feeling disorientated, confused and anxious all over again. It was as though all those negative feelings, that were once under control, were now pouring out of my system. I went back to see my doctor and she told me that weaning myself off it had to be a much slower process. What was making me more upset was I was beginning to feel unmotivated and unhappy, when I shouldn't have been feeling that. I had stopped writing new and creative ideas for comedy and blogs in the notebook I carried around with me. David had made a comment that seeing me so unhappy was making him question if I couldn't make myself happy, how could he ever make me happy. I always explained that I knew I needed to have the self-love my parents never gave me and find it myself. I could tell he was down and didn't particularly want to be around me. After a row over literally nothing, which I had started just to let off some steam, I made the decision to write a letter to David. After all, he didn't even know about anything to do with the medication I had been on all those years. I hadn't even told anyone about the CBT I had. Only David knew I had gone, and he just thought I went so I could change my thought patterns, he wasn't aware of any deeper process or diagnosis that went along with the sessions. So, I wrote to him and openly discussed my feelings about the depression, PTS and anxiety I had suffered from. to Once I had explained everything, to why I behaved the way I did, the medication I had been taking and why I was acting so strange after deciding to come off it. I felt like a weight had been lifted off my chest. David on the other hand was disappointed I hadn't told him before, but he seemed to be clearer and more understanding about the situation. I never expected him to understand because he never suffered from anything like what I did, but it felt good knowing he knew my thoughts and feelings.

With those who don't suffer from depression, PTS or any mental issue will never understand, that it's a potentially life-long illness that has to be controlled and managed. From my experience, acknowledging the problem in the first place was a huge hill to climb, but dealing with the issues and recognising them was a great achievement for me, having spent my whole life being so closed-minded to it. It didn't matter what an individual had in life, what they looked like, what career or money they had; mental health, if broken made no difference, and that was what the media had starting to try and convey to help society and uneducated people understand.
I had written a poem for myself one dull Monday afternoon, while I had been working at the Masons. I felt it was important to send it to David to possibly help him understand my thoughts even more.

Treatment

> *A brain that's been tapped and tinkered is suddenly transformed.*
> *A soul that's been prodded and pulled is carefully put back in its place.*

Thoughts have been dusted and polished and put away
in their boxes.
A gut that been untangled, unknotted, instead now tied
in a bow.

Then the cogs in the wheel turn again.
A scar to the brain has split.
The crack in its box is on display.
A scratch on the soul wants remedy.

And the bow has been pulled undone
Agitation covers the gloss.
Murky thoughts cloud the vision.
The focus slips out the window,
And I'm left with the bleak.

So, I read over those words you wrote down.
I remember those lines that you told me.
It's a scab that wants scratching,
A boil that wants bursting.

The cogs get treated, tankard and oiled.
They turn back the other way again.
This will go on forever.

By the end of August, so many wonderful talented celebrities had died from cancer. Tracey's funeral was held in Sweden months earlier, but Uncle Joe held a memorial for her in Cheltenham. With no experience of death of someone I knew personally, I was still struggling to come to terms with the situation and that the day was even real. It was as though it wasn't really happening. It wasn't a real situation. I was acting completely normal on the outside, I was refusing to accept she was gone but thoughts of the inevitable kept creeping into my mind each day, growing stronger and darker until the thoughts started to take over my mind. I once read that 35% of people are terrified of WHEN they are going to die, whereas the 65% are terrified of HOW they are doing to die. For me it was neither. I just had the simple, incomprehensible fear of the inevitable. The lack of control, the fact that there's absolutely nothing I could ever do about it. There was nothing I could ever do to stop it. The terrifying dread that loomed over me, night and night that one day I would be nothing, for eternity.

I found a quote on a website called '*Uncommon Help*'. It was written by an anonymous person, but it was as though I had written it. It was exactly my fear. And I'm sure many other people's too.

"Fear of death. I forget about it sometimes; I might be at a party or having dinner with friends, and then it hits me all over again. I'm going to die! I don't know when, but I do know it will happen sometime. One day I won't be here, none of us will. I feel frightened, sad, and immediately stop enjoying myself. What's the point? Because I'll be dead one day anyway! It happens at night sometimes, too—I become acutely aware, not just a thought, but a strong feeling that one day I 'll be gone... forever."

I would be doing normal everyday tasks and in the back of my mind I would think that one day I wouldn't be there anymore, I would be apart from David, the world and all the beauty that was in it would be gone, forever. These thoughts consumed me, and I started to notice whenever I was in a good mood, or felt good, or happy, I couldn't enjoy those feelings of joy. I felt I couldn't feel good or happy because death and sadness came in ahead. I was punishing myself for feeling good which had been going on for far too long. After reading that extract, that very moment I realised I hadn't been living a fulfilled life with these thoughts I had day in and day out. It was then, I referred myself to have the psychotherapy I was ready to receive.

Budapest, Hungary, where a lot of my family were born and raised. I was a little embarrassed to tell people I had never been to Hungary before but the opportunity to go just never came about. I either didn't have the money to go or my Hungarian family members had always visited England. I had lost touch with them after my mother and her father had fallen out and it wasn't until Facebook was launched that all my Hungarian family members thought me and my mother were

167

dead. Her father had told them all we had died in a car accident years earlier after the family fell out when I was twelve. It was quite a shock when all my cousins had found me on Facebook considering they thought I was dead.

When I finally got the chance to go to Hungary, I was booked to perform comedy at one of the biggest festivals in the world, The Sziget festival in Budapest. I jumped at the chance. Not only would I get a chance to perform in front of a huge international crowd, but I would also be paid to be doing something I enjoyed in a beautiful country instead of standing around a car show room sneakily writing and forming comedy ideas on the sly.

The promoter who had booked me for this big gig had seen me do my audition piece for *Britain's Got Talent* at the Hen & Chickens Theatre. He had a reputation for being a little flirtatious, maybe a little inappropriate with females, but nothing I couldn't handle. A hand on the leg, and some innuendo comments, my forced a smile and a change of subject put him straight. Considering he was pushing 60 and I always dropped David's name into the conversation, he knew there was no chance of anything happening. And anyway, as flirty as he was, he never physically made a pass at me and we did get on. From booking me in the past, I was grateful to be booked for such a big gig as The Sziget festival.

My flight was booked to leave two days after Tracey's Funeral. I was exhausted and drained as I turned up to the airport, takeaway coffee in one hand and small luggage case in the other. The promoter text to say he was running late.

After thirty minutes of waiting, he arrived, flustered and stressed as he came bowling in, laptop open, balanced on one hand, suitcase spilling out items in the other. He was trying to locate his tickets from the laptop, whilst packing and walking at the same time, until everything flew out everywhere. As I helped him scramble up his miniature bottles of shampoo and deodorant, I found his unruly stress was stressing me out. As we were running out of time to board, and he still couldn't find his ticket, he let me go on ahead of him and as I walked through customs, I turned to see him on his knees packing and cursing to himself. He eventually boarded the plane, spilling paperwork and a newspaper over my head as he sat down next to me.

The comedy show was held in a large tent in the heart of the festival. The comics and I put on a great show with the Hungarians in the audience appreciating jokes I told taking the piss out myself being half-Hungarian. It felt even better when young girls approached me after wanting their photo taken with me. It felt so good to be seen by strangers as someone they could now relate, accept and possibly even look up to.

After the show I and the other comedians were taken to a VIP party where I met very established comedians and was introduced to Ambassadors of England, Hungary and America. Groupies, fans and socialites stood around the wealthy men whilst name droppers and party people with selfie sticks and gossips gathered around the other comics and all I wanted was to get out of there.

The promoter urged me to flirt with the Ambassador of California who was a balding, sweaty overweight old man who had told me not once, but twice that he hung out with Michael Douglas. When I told the promoter I was not prepared to flirt with such a person, he drunkenly snarled, "And this is why you haven't made it." As I found myself surrounded by people, suddenly I felt alone and isolated wondering if this was a life I really wanted to lead.

When leaving to go home, our flights were at 4a.m. I was tired but alert because yet again, the promoter hadn't printed out his tickets. So once again, I went on ahead. I just wanted to get home and considering I had my ticket ready, I wasn't prepared to miss my flight. I was happy to have gigged in Hungary for such a huge event but all I wanted to do was go home to David.

Two weeks later, I was invited to a BAFTA comedy charity event by the same promoter. I was reluctant to go, but he said it would be great for my profile and there would be some high-end promoters, comedians and contacts there to meet. I wanted the chance to mingle with some fellow comics, so I accepted and felt positive. Maybe Hungary was just one bad experience and I decided to move on from it and take the opportunity.

When I turned up at the BAFTA building, with its grand beautiful grand entrance, there were a few famous comics roaming the room, however they were heavily outnumbered by the rich corporate businessmen that sat at tables, ready to auction to win tickets for comedy nights and events. My heart sank. To place a huge fat cherry on the top of the cake, the promoter who had invited me had also invited four other females to sit around him on his table. I felt like an accessory as I sat there listening to him crack jokes and put his hand on my knee every two minutes.

As we sat and ate an expensive three course meal, the promoter dropped a large knob of butter down his jacket, with one of the other girls he had invited, who was new to comedy, quickly got up and eagerly wiped it clean off for him. As I sat grimacing, I knew I didn't want to gig for him again. I planned to leave early and just before I got the chance to go, as I said my goodbyes to him, he tried to get me to stay and urged me to talk to the rich businessmen. I told him there and then I wasn't interested and left with a lovely girl I had got chatting to during the drinks who wanted to leave too. I never wanted to be so far away from the industry as much as I did that day.

The Hungarian festival and BAFTA experience opened my eyes to a part of a world in the entertainment industry I just didn't want to be around. I found myself withdrawing from the business and I suddenly found myself cancelling gigs. I had gigs booked in Prague the following month, with my face already printed on the posters and tickets were on sale, I told the company I couldn't make it. I had never wanted to go to something as much as this. I didn't want to experience the same situation that I had in Hungary all over again. I knew how unprofessional it looked on my part, but I just couldn't bring myself to go. It was then that I decided to step away from the comedy world.

Diary Extract September 21, 2016

Writing so many notes, poem blogs, thoughts and feelings about my experiences over the years from starting stand-up comedy, dealing with depression and experiencing the pain and anguish of losing David made me put them all together to form a book. My memoir. I want to share my story so people can either relate to them, laugh at them, or just enjoy the highs and lows of my experiences. Most of all, I want to inspire people, young and old to show them that if you can find some belief within yourself, you can be achieve anything. Even with mental health issues, eventually you can get where you want to be. Never let anyone tell you that you can't do something, even if it's a little different, or eccentric. Do what YOU want to do and what makes you happy. Remember that those who tell you that you can't achieve something, know that it is their problem. Most of all, there is no time limit – if you can't figure out where you are meant to be in life, give it time, it will come. This is the message I want to send to people who read my book.

It wasn't until after I had all these different encounters and experiences in a short amount of time, I had, in essence, learnt some of these valuable lessons in life. Since those dark times, I now believe that every human being should go through some pain and dark times in life, to inevitably become a true whole person that can grow emotionally, mentally and spiritually. Experience and lessons shape and test humans, sometimes to a point we find an inner strength we never knew we had. Growing in character and looking at your own emotional depth ultimately makes people better people.

When I look back at myself before 2009 to today, I can see how far I've come as a human being and I feel really proud of myself. My past is my past and it feels like an entire life time ago or even someone else' life. I am not the person I was, and I have grown into a new character, appreciating things and seeing light through dark times. Of course, the old me has crept through at times, I still feel fear when I get that pang at the thought of losing David, or I doubt my ability to do anything good, or when I still get really wound up about such unimportant things, but I'm only human after all. I'm aware that even now I still push away positive opportunities away and question my self-worth, but fundamentally, I have become aware of this and I have to try daily to tell myself I am a good person and I do deserve good things and not to be afraid of change in life. Terrified of the unknown, thinking it was so much easier to have things go wrong for me because that's what I deserved and that's what I was used to. It was easier to feel shit as I felt comfortable that way. I even questioned if I had made excuses to put the comedy on hold. It was becoming a profession and a prominent part of my life and I had chosen to put it at arm's length like so many things.

CBT, time and experience had taught me to realise that I don't have to throw it all away when something good comes my way in life. I've learnt to open up a little bit more and accept love, and let good things gravitate towards me even if it made me feel vulnerable. Giving love and showing affection doesn't make me weak, it makes me strong.

There are things you can be certain about, things you are in control of; your decisions and your actions to achieve what you want in life. But then there are those times when you are certain about something and it turns out differently. But it can be for the better. 'Never say never' is my new motto in life. You never know what great things are coming your way.

I want to give people advice from the mistakes I have made and the things I have learnt. Be true to yourself is something I would tell people. Be real and honest with yourself, about who you are and what is important in life. Do what you want in life and don't be afraid of what others think, because they are the ones who want to do it too. Being positive really does attract and create positive situations and good things fall into place.

I have been asked by a few people, over the last three years, a very valid question, 'If David hadn't have ever contacted me again, would I have gotten over him?' I have two answers to that. The first is: No. I knew I would always love him no matter what. Simple as that. But that leads to the second answer, I knew all along that moving on and loving someone else, second best wasn't an option. Settling for a second love was never right for me. And I knew David would always be in contact with me. It's a strange feeling I can't really explain, but my gut, my intuition, my heart, whatever it was, I knew he would come back. And he did.

Where Is Naomi Now

Naomi is now a professional writer with a large portfolio of work. From writing the content of a wedding photographers' website, to articles, features and blogs on mental health and other interesting subjects.

She appeared in an eye-opening documentary about sexual harassment which aired on ITV and is currently writing a second book since completing a course in Journalism.

Naomi took the opportunity and referred herself to receive psychotherapy, which started in October 2018. She has learnt that life isn't just about being happy, but about actually embracing that happiness.

Naomi never found out who made those 'Keep calm but Naomi Hefter defriended me' items, and in case you were wondering, she was fired from her last reception job making it 37 times. She has no plans to get fired as a writer.

Most importantly, Naomi and David are engaged to be married, the wish she had always dreamt of.

About Naomi

Naomi Hefter, living proof you should never judge a book by its cover, was born in Cheltenham, studied in Worcester and stopped off in Bristol before moving to the city of London amongst the neon lights.

She is a natural born writer and poet, a seven-year stand-up comedian, presenter and model who also plays the flute. She has an endless bucket list of things to experience, including meeting Jim Carrey, hugging a tiger and wearing neon clothes in Tokyo. With a passion for theatre, true crime and '90s trance music, Naomi also lives for eccentric fashion, modern art and anything from the '60s and '70s.

If you don't find Naomi planning her weekends with lists and ideas or flicking through a Warhol book, you may find her in the bath eating a Big Mac or dancing at a rave.

Ingram Content Group UK Ltd.
Milton Keynes UK
UKHW020231050423
419646UK00001B/6

9 781788 780650